AN ARMY WIFE'S C

WITH HOUSEHOLD HINTS AND HOME REMEDIES

ALICE KIRK GRIERSON
1828 - 1888

Compiled and Edited by
> MARY L. WILLIAMS
> FORT DAVIS NATIONAL HISTORIC SITE

Introduction by
> ALICE KIRK GRIERSON
> AND
> SARAH JOY GRIERSON

Sketches by
> ETTA M. KOCH

ALICE KIRK GRIERSON

Alice Kirk, oldest of the twelve children of John and Susan Bingham Kirk, was born in Youngstown, Ohio, in 1828. As the daughter of a wealthy and prominent merchant, Alice received an excellent education and was an honor student at the Huron Institute in Milan, Ohio. During her early teens, she became acquainted with Benjamin H. Grierson, a fine lad only two years her senior, who was destined to become her one and only love. Ben was a member of a minstrel troop which performed in and around Youngstown, and Alice, because of her great interest in music, was often found in attendance at the group's recitals. Their mutual love for music fostered a deep and lasting affection between them, and despite parental disapproval they were married September 24, 1854. In 1855 their first child, Charles Henry, was born.

At first, Ben earned his living as a musician. He taught music, wrote and arranged pieces for bands and orchestras, and often gave recitals and concerts. When the Civil War broke out Ben abandoned his musical career and joined the 10th Illinois Infantry. Despite lack of military training, he was an excellent soldier and by the end of the war had attained the rank of Major General of Volunteers.

During the war, Alice lived at the Grierson homestead in Jacksonville, Illinois. Her time during long periods of separation from her husband was spent in devotedly caring for her young and growing family. Two more sons and a daughter were born between 1856 and 1865.

In April, 1866, Ben was mustered out of the Volunteers and two months later joined the Regular Army. With the rank of Colonel and commander of the newly-formed 10th Cavalry, Ben had at last found his vocation. Alice was destined to follow the guidon westward until her death in 1888.

Our grandmother died before we were born, but the love and respect that Charles, our father, had for his entire family was evident to us. We take pride in knowing that a portion of her frontier Army life is being preserved.

ALICE KIRK GRIERSON
SARAH JOY GRIERSON
Los Angeles, California
1972

Library of Congress Catalog Card Number: 72-91099

Standard Book Number: 0-911408-27-4

Manufactured in China

AN ARMY WIFE'S COOKBOOK

Alice Kirk Grierson was not the typical army wife of the late 19th century, for she rarely had to endure the extreme hardships associated with frontier army life. Coming from a wealthy family, and usually living beyond her husband's paycheck, she seldom did without necessities or luxuries. She infrequently moved with the army, but would visit family and friends back East until the packing, unpacking and setting up of new quarters had been completed by servants.

Mrs. Grierson usually employed two full-time servants and often hired three or four. One servant had the responsibility of cooking for the family. A new cook was either shown how to prepare desired dishes, or Alice would copy recipes from her personal cookbook for the servant to use. This may explain why today the pages of Mrs. Grierson's cookbook are in such good condition. From all appearances, her book only occasionally was used in the kitchen.

In 1968, Mrs. Grierson's cookbook was donated to the National Park Service at Fort Davis National Historic Site by Mrs. Edith Flynt Phillips of Dallas, Texas. Mrs. Phillips' uncle, the owner of a second-hand store in Marfa, Texas, obtained the book in 1935 when George Grierson, youngest of Ben and Alice's children, set about cleaning out the family properties at Fort Davis.

Alice Grierson kept her recipes in a bound book having lined blue pages. Most of the recipes are written in her hand. The book also contains household hints and recipes clipped from newspapers and magazines, and recipes from friends and relatives. All together there are approximately six hundred recipes, however many are duplicates. For instance, there are thirteen recipes for lemon pie, and nineteen for muffins. Over one-half of the recipes are for desserts. The book has very few recipes for main dishes or vegetables. Some recipes, like "Cake Without Eggs," and "Doughnuts Without Eggs," reflect the ingenuity of a frontier wife during times when certain ingredients were not readily obtainable.

As was the custom, Alice merely listed ingredients and brief preparation statements. Through the generous help of National Park Service wives of the Southwest Region and their friends, over one hundred of her recipes were tested and preparation procedures noted. In this edition, Mrs. Grierson's recipes are printed in brown ink. Underneath, in black ink, are their modern adaptations and methods of preparation. The original recipes are printed exactly as they were found with old spelling forms and punctuation marks being retained. In testing, the old recipes were followed as closely as possible. Changes were made only when absolutely necessary to improve either texture or taste. Some of Mrs. Grierson's recipes tested beautifully the first time around, while others needed revision and retesting.

Researching background materials for this book brought to light many interesting and delightful stories related by army women who recorded their adventures in journals and diaries. Although Mrs. Grierson wrote letters to relatives and friends, she did not keep a day by day account of the years she spent in the West. Thus, some of the culinary adventures described by other officers' wives are included in an attempt to give the reader a glimpse into the kitchen of a frontier army wife.

In addition to her recipes, a sampling of Mrs. Grierson's home remedies and housekeeping hints is included. They are entertaining to read as well as challenging to try.

—Mary L. Williams
Fort Davis National Historic Site

Coffee mill

SOUPS

As the making of soup was often thought to be a laborious chore, enough was made to last for several days. Soup, as in Mrs. Grierson's day, is still considered essential in a full course dinner. It may be served as a main dish or beverage, as well as a first course. Hot and hearty soups are a warm welcome in winter, and light, even chilled soups are enjoyed in summer. Mrs. Grierson's CLAM CHOWDER is an excellent main course dish, and her SIMPLE HOT WEATHER SOUP is a welcome substitute for coffee or tea.

Many times soups were not made from specific recipes, but from beef stock and whatever vegetables one might have on hand. In some homes, a soup pot was left on the back of the stove and each day a few vegetables or meat trimmings were added. Although the days of large soup pots and soup tureens have somewhat disappeared, to many of us there is no more cheerful sight on a cold day than a kettle of soup simmering on the kitchen stove.

Soup tureen

LOTTIE'S CURRY BISQUE

One quart can of tomatoes
one quart of milk
one dozen whole cloves
one heaping teaspoon of salt
one bay leaf
one heaping teaspoon of celery seed
one heaping teaspoon of caraway seed

several sprigs of parsley
one large onion sliced
4 even tablespoons of flour
1 even tablespoon of butter
½ teaspoon curry powder
¼ teaspoon of sugar

Put on tomatoes to boil. When hot add a lump of soda the size of a pea, then add salt, cloves, bay leaf, celery seed, caraway seed, parsley, and onion. Let boil until tomato is cooked all to pieces, some 20 or 35 minutes. Strain through a medium coarse strainer, rubbing it well. Have milk just luke warm and add. Put on to boil up, then add the flour and butter creamed, then the tiny bit of sugar, and last the curry powder. It should be creamy and smooth, thicker than soup and the color of salmon.

2 cups canned tomatoes
⅛ teaspoon baking soda
1 teaspoon salt
1 teaspoon caraway seed
1 teaspoon celery seed
⅛ teaspoon powdered (dry) clove
1 teaspoon parsley flakes

⅓ cup chopped onion
2 cups milk
1-½ teaspoon margarine or butter
2 tablespoons flour
⅛ teaspoon sugar
¼ teaspoon curry powder

Bring tomatoes to a boil. Add the next seven ingredients and stir well. Let boil until tomatoes separate, about 20 minutes. Strain through a coarse strainer, rubbing well. Heat milk to lukewarm. Add tomato mixture and bring to a boil. Cream flour and margarine. Add small amount of tomato-milk mixture until flour and margarine make a thin paste. Add to tomato-milk mixture. Add sugar and curry powder. Simmer 5 minutes. Makes 4 to 6 servings.

This elegant first course dish can be made early, refrigerated, and reheated at serving time.

When making soup *"success largely depends upon the cooking and skimming, and failure is generally owing to rapid boiling and neglecting to skim the pot. If the soup is allowed to simmer, the allowance of water given in the recipes will not require replenishing. If, however, it is allowed to boil hard, the water will evaporate fast and require replenishing with boiling water. Fast boiling drives off much of the aroma of the ingredients."*
Manual for Army Cooks, Revised Edition, 1883.

CLAM CHOWDER

Take ½ pound of pork and fry it out, or ¼ pound of pork and ¼ pound of butter, to which add 3 pints of water. 2-½ pounds potatoes. 3 onions. Boil them all together, and when the potatoes are well done, open and add the contents of a can of clams, chopped into fine pieces (the size of an Indian corn). 8 crackers and one pint of good milk. Let it simmer together five minutes and it will be ready for the table.

¼ pound salt pork, chopped
¼ pound butter or margarine
3 pints water
10 medium potatoes
3 small onions, sliced
1 pint half and half (milk and cream)

2 cans minced clams
8 crackers, large squares, crumbled
1 tablespoon salt
½ teaspoon pepper

Fry the salt pork in butter until lightly browned. Add water, potatoes, and onions and cook until the potatoes are tender. Add the clams, half and half, salt, pepper, and crackers. Simmer 5 minutes. Pour immediately into large, warmed soup bowls. Makes 12 to 16 servings.

PARKER HOUSE TOMATO SOUP

Make 2 quarts beef stock, cut up 2 quarts of tomatoes, 1 turnip, 1 carrot, 1 onion cut fine. Boil all together 1 hour, strain and set away. Take 4 ounces butter, 2 spoons flour, put in a saucepan and heat until brown, stirring all the time. Turn this into the soup, add 2 spoons fine sugar, salt and pepper to taste; boil 5 minutes and skim.

Mrs. Choate adds these suggestions. 1 can tomatoes will do very well. I take beef bone and boil all the day before I wish to use it. Large spoonful butter to one of flour is sufficient for the thickening.

We did not change any of the ingredients, but our method of preparation varied slightly from the original. Simmer the vegetables in the beef broth for one hour. Strain. Melt 4 ounces of butter or margarine in a saucepan. Stir in 2 tablespoons of flour and cook until mixture browns, stirring constantly. Stir flour mixture into the strained broth. Add 2 teaspoons sugar, 1 teaspoon salt, and ¼ teaspoon pepper. Simmer 5 minutes. Makes 6 servings.

MRS. BILLING'S TOMATO SOUP WITHOUT MEAT

1 pint tomatoes, 1 quart water, 1 pint milk, ½ teaspoon soda, 4 soda crackers rolled, butter, salt, and pepper to taste. Boil 20 minutes. Boil water and tomatoes together. Add milk and soda, then crackers and condiments.

1 large can tomatoes
1 tablespoon Instant Minced
  Onions
½ cup water
1 pint milk
½ teaspoon baking soda

4 soda crackers, rolled
2 tablespoons butter
¾ teaspoon salt
⅛ teaspoon pepper

Place tomatoes in a saucepan. Add minced onion and water and cook over medium heat for about 10 minutes. Stir occasionally to break up tomatoes. Add the other ingredients and bring mixture to a boil. Boil one minute and serve piping hot. Makes 4 servings.

SIMPLE HOT WEATHER SOUP

A good hot weather soup is made from rice, with beef extract and seasoning. Cook two tablespoonfuls of the rice in a quart of water, with a small onion peeled and chopped and one bay leaf. Cook slowly thirty minutes. Take out the bay leaf, and add two teaspoonfuls of beef extract. Season to taste with salt and white pepper.

This light, mild-tasting soup is appropriate to serve in any season. We substituted 2 beef boullion cubes for the 2 teaspoons of beef extract, but followed the original recipe in all other details.

MISS CARSON'S METHOD OF CLARIFYING SOUP
From "The Western Rural" — October 13, 1883

From the top of the stock after cooling—take off fat. To each quart of stock, add the white and shell of one egg and a tablespoon of cold water, which she puts in the bottom of her stew pan, before she pours in the soup. As the soup heats, the white of the egg hardens and absorbs the fibrous bits of meaty substance. The albumin in the soup and any stray particles of blood will rise with the egg shell to the surface, where it can be skimmed off.

BREADS

Bread was probably the first prepared food man learned to make, and through the ages it has remained an indispensable part of his daily diet. A young girl living in the 19th century was taught the art of bread making at a tender age, and it would remain a daily or weekly duty for the rest of her life. It was a long and tedious chore and often took many hours. Dough was usually kneaded for a full half hour and then set on a shelf, under which a lighted coal-oil lamp had been placed, to rise overnight. Loaves were baked on the floor of the oven rather than on a rack. Often a piece of paper was placed over them to prevent browning too quickly. When nicely browned and hollow-sounding they were removed from the oven and wrapped in bread cloths to cool. If bread was baked in the morning, and hot bread was desired for the last meal of the day, a small amount of dough was saved and made into bread in late afternoon.

Baking of bread was a hard enough chore in the home, but its preparation while traveling was almost an insurmountable task. Elizabeth Burt, wife of Lieutenant Colonel Andrew G. Burt, in traveling from Fort Leavenworth, Kansas, to Fort Bridger, Utah, in 1866, remarked that the wagons never stopped long enough for bread to be baked except on Sundays. When one was traveling, even biscuits were difficult to prepare. Lydia Spencer Lane, wife of Lieutenant William B. Lane, U.S. Mounted Rifles, was forced to make her daily biscuits on top of a mess-chest. After she prepared the dough she would pound it with a long-necked bottle, using the neck as a sort of handle. As she had only a dutch oven in which to do all her cooking and baking, she recalled that it was a real feat to bake biscuits that didn't turn out the color of coal.

In preparing for the long journey to a new post in the West, many an army wife would purchase a rooster and a number of hens. A coop made for them could easily be strapped to the back of a wagon, and thus a family would be assured of its daily supply of fresh eggs To Frances M. A. Roe, wife of Lieutenant Fayette Roe, Third In

fantry, her chickens were her pride and joy. She had twenty-one
of them, and doted over them as if they were her children. Sometimes though, especially in remote areas where prices tended to be
high (eggs sold in the Colorado Territory in 1880 for $1.50 a dozen),
eggs were a luxury. The army wife then had to make certain adjust-
ments in her recipes. One recipe in this section — DOUGHNUTS
WITHOUT EGGS—reflects her ingenuity at not letting the lack
of a basic ingredient prevent her family from enjoying a favorite
food.

Conestoga wagon

12

JULIA BUCKMASTER'S WHITE BREAD

Boil 3 medium size potatoes in one quart of water. Mash and strain through a colander. Add the water in which they were boiled. When cool add sufficient flour to make a stiff batter, one yeast cake after soaking in a little water, one tablespoon of white sugar, one half or more teaspoon of salt. Let stand until morning. Boil one pint sweet milk to which add one teaspoon of lard and one of butter, one tablespoon sugar. Let come to a boil and cool— then add flour and sponge. Let rise from 3 to 4 hours and knead into loaves. Rise until pans are full and bake—an hour.

3 medium size potatoes	1/4 teaspoon salt
1 quart water	1 cup evaporated milk
14 to 15 cups flour, sifted	1 cup water
2 pkg. dry yeast (1/4 oz. each)	2 teaspoons margarine
1 tablespoon sugar	1 tablespoon sugar

Peel, slice, and boil potatoes in 1 quart water until tender. Pour potatoes and water into blender. Blend until smooth. Cool. Sprinkle yeast on potato mixture. Stir in enough flour to make stiff batter (about 10 cups), salt, and 1 tablespoon sugar. Cover and let stand overnight. To evaporated milk add 1 cup water, margarine, and remaining sugar. Warm milk mixture until margarine melts. Cool to room temperature and add to potato-flour mixture. Stir in enough of the remaining flour (about 4 to 5 cups) to make a soft dough. Mix with electric mixer on high speed for 3 minutes. Turn into greased bowl, cover and let rise until doubled, about 2 hours. When dough has doubled, punch down and turn out on floured surface. Knead for about 10 minutes. Form into 5 loaves and place into greased loaf pans. Cover and let rise until doubled. Bake in a 400° oven for 40 minutes. Butter top of each loaf upon removal from oven. Makes 5 loaves or a week's bread supply.

YEAST

It has been a good many years since compressed yeast replaced home-made liquid yeast, but in Mrs. Grierson's time it was just becoming available. The potato was the basic ingredient of all home-made yeast. Some yeasts would never sour, while others had to be used within a week. The yeast was usually kept in a yeast jug and often measured in gills. A gill is equal to eight large tablespoons and today is more associated with the measurement of wine.

The next bread recipe originally called for one-half gill of home-made yeast. Instead, we substituted two packages of dry yeast, but have included a yeast recipe for those who would like to try it.

RECIPE FOR MAKING YEAST

Boil one pint of hops (in a bag) for two hours in a gallon of water. Peel one quart of potatoes and boil with the hops, one-half hour before the hops are done. Then pour the gallon of water from the hops upon a pint of flour, or perhaps a little more, would be better. Add the potatoes after being well mashed to this while hot, and one teacup of salt, one teacup of sugar and three large spoonfuls of ginger. When sufficiently cold add yeast to raise it. The yeast should be kept free from air and in a cool place.

BUTTERMILK BREAD

1 pint buttermilk. Enough flour to make a tolerably stiff batter. Add half gill of yeast or let rise five or six hours. If you make over night you need not add the yeast, but put in instead a table-spoonful white sugar. In the morning stir into the sponge a tea-spoonful soda dissolved in hot water, little salt, or two tablespoons melted butter. Work in just flour enough to handle the dough comfortably. Knead well. Make into loaves and let rise until light. This makes very white wholesome bread.

1 pint buttermilk	1 teaspoon baking soda
8 cups flour, sifted	2 tablespoons hot water
2 pkg. dry yeast ($\frac{1}{4}$ oz. each)	2 teaspoons salt
$\frac{1}{4}$ cup warm water	2 tablespoons butter

Heat the buttermilk until it is hot enough to melt the butter. Stir in butter and salt. Remove from heat and cool. Dissolve yeast in $\frac{1}{4}$ cup warm water and add to milk mixture. Dissolve baking soda in 2 tablespoons hot water, let cool, and add to milk mixture. Add half of the flour and beat until smooth. Add rest of the flour as needed to make a smooth dough that cleans the bowl. Turn out onto floured bread-board and knead 8-10 minutes. Turn into greased bowl, cover and let rise until doubled. Punch down and form into 2 loaves. Place in greased loaf pans and let rise until doubled. Bake at 400° for about 50 minutes or until lightly browned and done. (Incidentally, we tried this using sugar and no yeast, and it was a complete flop.)

MRS. E.'S SODA BISCUITS

1 quart flour, 2 heaping tablespoonfuls lard, 2 cups sweet milk, or you can take can milk, 1 teaspoonful soda, 2 teaspoonfuls cream of tarter, 1 teaspoonful salt. Rub soda and cream of tarter into flour dry. Next the lard. Lastly the milk. Work with as little handling as possible. The dough should be very soft. Cut more than half inch thick and bake in a quick oven.

We decided to cut this recipe in half, as the original makes about 30 biscuits. We also used more shortening, remembering that often a tablespoonful in the "good old days" was quite heaping as compared with the level amount we use today.

2 cups flour	1 teaspoon cream of tartar
½ teaspoon baking soda	2 tablespoons lard or margarine
½ teaspoon salt	¾ to 1 cup milk

Sift dry ingredients together. Add shortening and cut into flour mixture. Add milk, a little at a time, stirring with a fork. Add as much of the milk as necessary to make a very soft dough. Roll out ½ inch thick and cut with a small biscuit cutter. Bake at 425° for 15-20 minutes. Makes 15 biscuits.

BUNS

2-½ cups of milk, 1 cup of yeast, 1 of sugar, flour to make a batter to rise over night. In the morning add a cup of sugar, 1 cup of butter, a little soda, knead well and rise again. When perfectly light, roll out, cut into cakes and then rise light before baking.

As with the soda biscuits, we also cut this recipe in half.

1 cup milk, scalded	1 package dry yeast
½ cup + 2 tablespoons sugar	¼ cup warm water
½ cup butter	4 cups flour, sifted
¾ teaspoon baking soda	

Combine milk with 2 tablespoons sugar. Dissolve yeast in ¼ cup warm water. Let set 5 to 10 minutes. Add yeast and 2 cups flour to milk mixture. Beat for one minute. Cover and let rise until doubled, about 45 minutes. When dough has doubled, punch it down and add butter, baking soda, and remaining sugar. Mix thoroughly. Add enough of the remaining flour (about 2 cups) to make a soft dough. Turn onto lightly floured breadboard. Pat or roll the dough to a thickness of about ⅓ inch. Cut with a biscuit cutter and place on greased cookie sheet. Cover and let rise until doubled. Bake at 425° for 15 minutes. Makes about 24 buns.

TENDER CRUST—If the crust of bread is wished tender, as soon as the loaves are taken out of the oven, wrap them in a wet cloth rung from cold water, and then over it a dry towel.

MUFFINS, SOUR MILK

1 pint sour milk, piece butter size of an egg, melted, salt to taste, 1 teaspoon soda put dry into milk. Add flour enough to make a stiff batter. Bake in tins, the batter stiff enough for spoon to stand up.

Through trial and error, we found that these "muffins" are actually very fine biscuits and should be prepared as such.

2 cups sour milk
4 tablespoons butter, melted
3 cups flour

1 teaspoon salt
1 teaspoon baking soda, put dry into milk

Mix together the milk (to which baking soda has been added), butter and salt. Blend well. Stir flour into the liquid mixture. Blend thoroughly. Roll dough out on floured breadboard, just as if you were making biscuits. Cut with a biscuit cutter, and place on greased cookie sheets. Bake in a 400° oven for 15 to 20 minutes. Makes about 3 dozen.

bread raiser

LOYAL BISCUITS

Mrs. Billings — Alton, Illinois

3 cups flour, 1 cup sweet milk, 3 eggs, little sugar, butter the size of an egg, 3 spoonfuls baking powder. Bake as muffins.

3 cups flour, sifted	4 tablespoons sugar
1 cup milk	4 tablespoons butter, melted
3 eggs	3 teaspoons baking soda

Sift dry ingredients into a bowl. Add milk, eggs, and melted butter and stir just until dry ingredients are thoroughly moistened. Batter should still be lumpy. Fill buttered muffin pans 2/3 full. Bake in a 375° oven for 20 to 25 minutes. Makes 30 biscuits. (This recipe may easily be reduced to make only 10 or 20 biscuits.)

DOUGHNUTS WITHOUT EGGS

2 quarts flour, 1 pint milk, 1 full cup sugar, and a piece of butter size of an egg. Scald milk and when tepid, add sugar and butter, half cup yeast, and half spoon soda. Pour this in the center of the flour, using enough flour to make a sponge. Let rise over night in a warm place. If light in the morning, sprinkle in whatever spice preferred. Knead in remainder of flour, then knead 15 or 20 minutes. Roll thin, cut with biscuit cutter. Let stand 5 minutes and fry.

2 cups milk	4 tablespoons margarine
1 cup sugar	6 cups flour, sifted
½ teaspoon baking soda	½ teaspoon cinnamon
2 cakes compressed yeast or	½ teaspoon nutmeg
2 pkg. active dry yeast dissolved in ¼ cup warm water	

Scald milk and then add sugar and margarine. Cool mixture to lukewarm. Add yeast and baking soda and enough flour to make a sponge (4-½ to 5 cups). Cover and let rise in a warm place until doubled. Combine the spices and remaining flour and knead into mixture. Knead about 5 minutes. Cover and let rise until doubled. Fry doughnuts in hot deep fat (350° on a frying thermometer) until golden brown on both sides. Drain on absorbent paper. Dust with confectioners' sugar.

RUSK

Mrs. Johnson — Alton, Illinois

1 cup of sugar, 2 eggs, butter the size of two eggs, 2 cups of milk, 6 cups of flour, 6 teaspoonfuls of baking powder, raisins and spices if you choose. Bake at once. This makes two loaves.

Rusks were much more popular one hundred years ago than they are today. Rusk, a type of sweet bread or cake, could be made very simply like the present day zwieback, or like a light, spicy fruit bread. Mrs. Grierson's recipe makes a deliciously flavored light bread. In it we used 1-½ cup raisins and 1-½ teaspoons of ground cinnamon.

Cream the butter (margarine may be used instead), add sugar and beat until mixture is light and fluffy. Beat in eggs one at a time and blend well. Stir in raisins. Sift flour, baking powder, and cinnamon together. Add sifted ingredients to the creamed mixture, alternately with milk, beginning and ending with flour. Turn batter into two well-greased loaf pans and bake in a 350° oven for 30 to 40 minutes or until done.

GINGERBREAD

E. L. King, Jacksonville

1-½ cups molasses, into which, stir until it foams, 3 even teaspoons of soda, 1 cup sugar, 1 scant cup of butter, 2 large eggs, not beaten separately, 1-½ cups sour milk, ginger to taste, 3-½ cups flour. Bake either in small cakes or in sheets. Part lard can be used if butter is scant.

Cream butter and sugar together. Beat in eggs. Stir baking soda into molasses and mix until foamy. Add molasses mixture to creamed mixture. Sift flour and ginger together, and add to creamed mixture, alternately with the sour milk. Pour batter into two greased cake pans and bake in a 375° oven for 35 minutes or until done.

STALE BREAD — It is not generally known that stale bread, when immersed in cold water for a moment or two, and re-baked for about an hour, is in every respect equal to newly-baked bread.

VEGETABLES

The army wife was usually limited to vegetables she raised herself or was lucky enough to purchase from a nearby farmer. They were simply prepared and often, in a poor growing season, a family would have the same kind served over and over again. If possible, vegetables were hung out to dry during harvest months and then stored in cool bins for use during the winter. Katherine Gibson, wife of Captain Francis M. Gibson of the Seventh Cavalry, remembered being quite upset to find that she could not readily get fresh beans, lettuce, or spinach upon her arrival at Fort Lincoln, Dakota Territory, in the late 1870's. She was quickly informed that beans sold for fifty cents a quart, lettuce was very scarce, and spinach was practically unheard of. Similar situations occurred at almost every army post in the West, and Mrs. Grierson must have experienced many of the same feelings at not being able to secure her favorite vegetables. We find that her cookbook contains very few recipes for preparing them, but some of the more flavorsome are included here.

chopping set

GREEN CORN OMELET

Grate the corn from 12 ears of corn, boiled. Beat up 5 eggs, stir them with the corn, season with salt and pepper and fry the mixture brown. Fry in small cakes with a little flour and milk, stirred in to form a batter.

We found this recipe more like one for corn fritters than for a corn omelet; nevertheless, the corn lover will not be disappointed in the result.

1 can whole kernel corn, drained
5 eggs, separated
1 cup flour
½ cup milk
salt and pepper to taste
1 teaspoon baking powder

Combine corn, flour, and baking powder and mix well. Beat yolks of eggs until thick and add to corn mixture with the milk. Beat whites of eggs until stiff and fold into the mixture. Drop by tablespoonfuls and fry in deep fat. Remove from pan and drain on paper towels.

FRIED TOMATOES AND RICE

Fry half a small cup of raw rice in hot lard 15 minutes. In another pan fry in drippings ¼ of a small onion, not an El Paso onion but a northern sized onion. Add ½ cup of tomato and let fry. Add hot water to the rice until the consistency of firm boiled rice. Add a little at a time put contents of the two pans together and serve in a hot dish with the toast if you like. Salt and pepper of course.

⅓ cup uncooked rice
¼ cup chopped onion
2 tablespoons cooking oil
½ cup cooked tomatoes
½ teaspoon salt
¼ teaspoon pepper
½ to 1 cup hot water
2 tablespoons bacon drippings

Cook the rice in cooking oil for 15 minutes, stirring frequently. In another pan cook chopped onion in bacon drippings. Add tomatoes, salt, and pepper to the onions and continue to cook for 2 or 3 minutes, stirring often. Add hot water to the rice, a little at a time, until it reaches consistency of firm boiled rice. Add rice to the tomatoes and serve. Makes 4 servings.

BOSTON BAKED BEANS

1 quart beans soaked over night. In the morning drain. Then cover with warm water, and add one pound of pork. Boil gently an hour. Then turn into a colander and rinse with cold water. Then put half of beans in bean pot. Then pork. Then the rest of beans. Pour over them one teaspoon of mustard, a tablespoon of salt, a tablespoon molasses mixed in a cup of water. Bake slowly ten hours adding water as it cooks away.

In attempting to determine what type beans could be used in preparation of this dish, we found that the traditional pea bean, long considered the proper bean for this Boston favorite, did not come from New England, but is native to California. Until migration of the pea bean from the west coast to the east coast in the late 1840's, the kidney bean was the common bean used in New England baking. In our preparation, we used dried navy beans. We did not alter the original recipe, merely using *salt* pork and *dry* mustard for the pork and mustard indicated. We baked the beans in a covered dish in a 250° oven for the full 10 hours. Makes 12 servings. For a little spicier flavor, add one medium peeled onion placed in the middle of the beans before baking.

Beans while an excellent food for the robust and healthy and for persons leading an active life, are considered unsuitable for persons of sedentary habits and for the invalid and convalescent.
—The Mess Officer's Assistant.

POTATO PUFFS

2 cups of cold mashed potatoes. Stir into this 2 tablespoons melted butter beaten to a cream, 2 well beaten eggs, one cup of cream or milk. Pour this into a deep dish and bake in quick oven.

Mash potatoes with a fork and work in about ½ cup milk. Add remaining milk and beaten eggs. Add melted butter last. Pour into a 1 quart casserole dish and bake in a 425° oven for 45 to 50 minutes. Makes 4 servings. For extra flavor combine potato mixture with one small onion, grated, and bake as directed.

Paring potatoes before boiling them is wasteful and should only be resorted to late in the spring, when the potato has commenced to sprout. If pared, they should be laid in cold water for a half hour before cooking.—Manual for Army Cooks, revised edition, 1883.

CAULIFLOWER

Boil cauliflower until tender, pouring off first water after five minutes cooking. Drain and roll each fleuret in sifted bread crumbs. Cover with beaten egg to which add two tablespoons water. Roll second time in crumbs and fry in deep fat. Serve on a folded napkin with parsley between the fleuret and tomato sauce in a separate dish.

Separate cauliflower into flowerets. Cook in 1 inch water and 1 teaspoon sugar for about 10 minutes or until tender. Drain. Dip each floweret into beaten egg (1 egg and 2 tablespoons water). Roll in fine bread crumbs and fry in hot oil (275°) for 1 minute or less. Drain on paper towels or napkins. Serve in bowl sprinkled with parsley flakes.

For the tomato sauce combine:

1 8-oz. can tomato sauce	2 teaspoons brown sugar
1 teaspoon Worcestershire sauce	1 teaspoon horseradish

Mix above ingredients thoroughly and heat in sauce pan. Serve in separate dish. A large tablespoon of sauce over each serving of cauliflower makes this an exceptionally fine vegetable dish. Makes 4 servings.

Lack of vegetables in the West was of great concern to the army wife. Many women who kept journals of their experiences made references to the poor quality or complete absence of vegetables. Elizabeth Burt in describing her new home at Fort Bridger, Wyoming Territory, in 1866, wrote the following: *In all the valley there was no garden and consequently we had no vegetables, unless they were brought from Salt Lake City, and this made them too expensive to indulge in, except on rare occasions.*

SCALLOPED ONIONS

Boil until tender the onions changing water twice. Pour over them one cup of milk and let scald. Then place in baking dish layers of onions, bread or crackers. Butter, pepper, and salt. Bake half hour.

Peel and slice 4 medium size onions. Cook, uncovered, in enough boiling salted water to cover onions, for about 10 minutes or until tender. Drain water off and pour 1 cup of milk over onions and scald. Remove onions from milk. In a small baking dish, arrange alternate layers of onions and bread crumbs, dotted with butter and salt and pepper. Pour the reserved milk over top layer and bake in a 375° oven for 30 minutes. Makes 4 servings.

Frontier housekeeping in the 19th century not only had many drawbacks, but often had many trying moments that an army wife would just as soon have preferred to forget. When Lydia Lane's husband was commanding Fort Union, New Mexico in 1867, she found herself in a position where she did quite a bit of entertaining. The following is a delightful account of one such occasion which did not turn out quite as successful as she might have liked:

One day I had cooked a dinner for a family of seventeen, including children. It was on the table, and I was putting the last touches to it preparatory to retiring to the kitchen. I could not sit down with my guests and attend to matters there at the same time. I was stooping over to straighten something when I heard an ominous crack above my head, and, before I could move, down fell half the ceiling on my back and the table, filling every dish with plaster to the top. The guests had just reached the dining-room door in time to see the catastrophe, and finding I was unhurt they retired until the debris was cleared away and a second dinner was prepared. Fortunately, I had plenty of food in reserve, and it was soon on the table and disposed of by my friends with apparent relish. I, in the solitude of my kitchen, could not do justice to the subject, so kept quiet.

MEATS AND MAIN DISHES

One primary problem faced by an army wife in the 19th century was the lack of variety in army rations. Beef, beef, and more beef was the constant complaint around many a western army post. It was no wonder that hunting of wild game became such a popular sport. Wild turkey, pheasant, goose, duck, and even buffalo were considered rare treats. Frances M. A. Roe, in writing about Christmas dinner at Fort Lyon, Colorado Territory, in 1871, remembered that the Post Trader sent all the way to St. Louis for turkeys, canned oysters, and celery. As there were no fresh vegetables at the fort except potatoes, and meat rations consisted entirely of beef, this was indeed a very special dinner and one that was remembered for a long time.

Army women learned quickly how to make delicious dishes out of practically nothing. Many times their specialties were really not what they pretended to be. Mrs. Roe, telling about a party held at the post in 1872, recalled that it was a great success despite the fact that some of the dishes were frauds. It seems that the chicken salad was not made with chicken, but rather with veal, and the turkey galantine was really prepared from wild goose.

Mrs. Grierson also faced this same challenge of trying to prepare a main dish that was a little unusual. She was delighted when her sons reached the age when they could hunt. In all of her letters to family and friends back East, she never mentioned the hardships encountered in obtaining certain products, but always commented on the number of pheasant and quail her sons had brought home from a day of hunting. Though the Griersons enjoyed wild game as often as they could obtain it, Mrs. Grierson's cookbook has no recipes for its preparation. Her main dish recipes are very few in number and we have included in this section all of those which tested successfully.

GREEN CHILLI STUFFED WITH MACARONI

Boil the macaroni in wine (Sherry) or in water and <u>season</u> with wine. Add a little clove, grated cheese, pepper and salt and stuff the chilli. Roll in egg beaten separately very light, and fry, or you can steam.

1 cup macaroni	¼ teaspoon salt
½ cup cooking sherry	¼ teaspoon pepper
⅛ teaspoon clove	6 chiles—long green variety
½ cup grated cheese	1 egg, separated
½ cup cooking oil	1 tablespoon flour

Boil macaroni in 2 quarts of boiling water to which cooking sherry has been added. Cook until tender. Rinse in cold water. Drain. Grate the cheese and add salt, pepper, and clove. Combine with macaroni. Peel chiles and remove membranes. Lay flat and fill each with about 1 tablespoon of the cheese-macaroni mixture. Fold ends together. Beat egg white until stiff. Add yolk and flour and beat until creamy. Roll chiles in mixture and place in moderately hot skillet to which ½ cup cooking oil has been added. Fry a few seconds on each side or until golden. Makes 3 servings.

STUFFED CABBAGE LEAVES

Boil some beef or veal or chicken in a little water for full seven hours or until the water will jelly. When meat is cold chop fine. Add to taste some red or green chilli, onion, potatoe (cooked) or crumbs, a little celery, pepper, and salt, a few raisins, all chopped, a little chopped turnip and parsley. Parboil fresh cabbage leaves. Roll up this mixture in little light rolls and tie in the leaves, and boil in the jelly saved from the meat. Or, mix jelly with the stuffing and <u>fry</u> the rolls.

2 pounds lean beef or stew meat	1 cup boiled potato, diced
1 head green cabbage	2 tablespoons turnip, cooked
½ cup chopped onion	and diced
¼ cup diced bell pepper	½ can (7-½ oz.) green chiles
¼ cup diced celery	1 teaspoon dried parsley flakes
4 tablespoons butter	salt and pepper to taste

Simmer meat in a small amount of seasoned (salted and peppered) water for several hours. Cool, chop fine and reserve the broth. Saute onion, pepper, and celery in the butter. Add chopped meat. Add potato, turnip, green chiles, salt and pepper to the meat mixture. Mix thoroughly and set aside. Remove cabbage leaves from head and immerse in boiling salted water. Cook for 2 minutes or until leaves are partially translucent and pliable. Do just a few leaves at a time. Remove from heat and drain. Place a tablespoon of meat mixture in the center of each leaf, fold like an envelope and secure with a toothpick. Place rolls in large pot, add broth, cover and simmer for 20 minutes or until cabbage leaves are tender. Makes 14 cabbage rolls. (We also tried this recipe using chicken, but it was not as tasty. Cabbage flavor overpowered that of the chicken.)

ALBÓNDIGAS (Ruvio)

One pound of tenderloin steak or a pound of chicken meat boiled and ground very fine, the yolks of three well beaten eggs, salt, pepper, onion, and chile mixed and beaten until creamy, one pound of the finest ground Mexican masa added, and beaten again, adding two or three whole cloves. Roll in little balls the size of marbles, and boil in the jelly from meat or water left. Make a white cream sauce and pour over them and garnish with parsley or cresses.

1 lb. round steak or chicken	1 onion
3 eggs, beaten	1 4-oz. can chopped green chili
2 teaspoons salt	1-½ cups Masa Harina
¼ teaspoon pepper	¼ teaspoon ground cloves

Boil meat in 4 to 6 cups salted water for about 1 hour. Remove gristle and bone and grind in meat grinder with onion. Add beaten eggs, chile, salt, pepper, and clove. Mix well. Add Masa Harina and blend with a spoon. If too dry, add a little water. Form into small balls and drop into simmering water left from first boiling. Cook 1 hour. Make a white sauce and pour over the drained balls. Garnish with parsley or grated cheese. Makes 4 to 6 servings.

Cooked meat balls may also be put into a 9-inch square pan, covered with 1 can mild enchilada sauce and sprinkled with grated cheese. Bake in a 350° oven for approximately 15 to 20 minutes or until cheese melts.

Spider

SPICED BEEF

Chop very fine the tough ends of two beef steaks. A piece of suet the size of half hen's egg. Season with pepper, salt, and very little nutmeg. Add two well beaten eggs, ½ pint dry bread rolled fine, ½ pint crackers rolled, 4 or 5 tablespoons cream, butter size of an egg. Make a long roll with flour. Bake in drippings pan with a little drippings. Cook until brown and turn over several times.

3 or 4 pounds lean meat, ground
1-½ tablespoons suet
1 teaspoon pepper
1 teaspoon salt
¼ teaspoon nutmeg
2 eggs, well beaten

1 cup fine bread crumbs
1 cup fine cracker crumbs
5 tablespoons cream
3 tablespoons butter
scant ¼ cup flour

Combine all ingredients except flour. Shape into a roll and roll in flour. Bake in a long pan with a little drippings at 350° for approximately 75 minutes. Makes 10 servings.

Although most army wives seemed to complain because they had nothing but beef, Lydia Spencer Lane was an exception. While at Fort Inge, Texas, in 1856, she longed for a good beef-steak instead of wild game. As there were few soldiers at the post, beef was issued only once a month, and Lydia soon grew tired of the abundant quail, antelope, and deer.

CODFISH BALLS

1 pint codfish. 10 potatoes. Boil together. Mash and add two eggs, milk if needed and a tablespoon butter. Mold in flour and fry.

1 pkg. shredded salted dried
    codfish
2-½ cups warm mashed potatoes
1 egg, beaten

1 teaspoon salt
¼ teaspoon pepper
cooking oil for frying

Cook dried codfish according to directions on package. Mix fish with potatoes, egg, salt and pepper. Drop from tablespoon into pan of hot fat ½ inch deep. Brown on both sides. Remove from heat and drain. Makes 4 servings.

MAYONNAISE OF CHICKEN AND CELERY

Marinate one pint of cold chicken. Cut in small cubes with three tablespoons of oil. One teaspoon and a half of lemon juice or vinegar and a little salt and paprika. When ready to serve drain the marinade off from chicken and mix with chicken one cup of crisp celery cut in bits, one cup of chestnuts cooked and cut in small pieces when cold. Add mayonnaise to hold the mixture together. Shape in a mound on a border of lettuce leaves, mark with mayonnaise with a pastry bag and tube pipe a design up in the mound. Finish with a tuft of lettuce on top.

The use of chestnuts makes this a rather unusual chicken salad. It is easy to prepare and very tasty. We used a 5-oz. can of chestnuts, chopped, and about ½ cup mayonnaise to two cups diced cold marinated chicken. Chopped onions and pickle may be added for extra flavor. Makes 4 servings.

RICE AND BACON

Parboil ¾ cup of rice in boiling water 5 minutes. Drain on a sieve. Pour boiling water over ¼ pound bacon. Drain. Cut in inch pieces. Saute to a light yellow. Add rice, 3 cups stock or water, pepper. Simmer until tender, then add a cup of well reduced tomato purée —which means tomatoes passed through a sieve and simmered until thick. Mix thoroughly. Turn into a mound on a dish and arrange curls of fried bacon around it.

1 cup rice	1 teaspoon salt
¼ pound thick-sliced bacon	1 can (6 oz.) tomato paste
1-½ cups water	5 slices bacon, fried in curls
¼ teaspoon pepper	

Cut bacon into 1 inch pieces, saute to a light yellow. Add all other ingredients except bacon curls. Bring mixture to a boil. Cover and reduce heat. Simmer for 25 minutes or until rice absorbs liquid. Mound rice on a plate. Garnish with bacon curls. Makes 5 servings.

COOKIES

In many "old time" cookbooks, cookies were not listed in a separate section, but merely included in the cake section. They were often referred to as small cakes, drop cakes, or sweet biscuits. They were small, usually flat, and like today's could be crisp or soft, thick or thin, plain, filled, or frosted.

Although there are more varieties of cookies than any other baked product, Mrs. Grierson's cookbook contains only a small handful of recipes and most of these are just entitled "cookies." The recipes are very similar to one another, the substitution of a different flavoring being their only minor difference. We have tried to include in this section some of the more unusual cookie recipes found in the original book. We hope you will find them as much fun to make as we did.

Cookie crock

CHOCOLATE COOKIES

Recipe from the Deaf and Dumb Institute, Jacksonville, Illinois

3 eggs, 2-½cups of pulverized sugar, 1 cake of Baker's Chocolate, ½ cup of sour cream, 1 cup butter, 1 teaspoon of soda, 2 of cream of tartar. Flavor with vanilla. Flour enough to roll out nicely. Beat butter and sugar to a cream first, then add the rest.

We used 3 squares unsweetened chocolate, 2 teaspoons vanilla, and 6 cups flour. We did not alter the quantities of other ingredients.

Melt chocolate over hot, but not boiling water. In a bowl, combine butter, sugar, and sour cream and cream until light. Beat in eggs, one at a time, and then add vanilla. Sift flour with baking soda and cream of tartar and stir into the creamed mixture alternately with melted chocolate. Roll about ¼ inch thick on a lightly floured board and cut with a small cookie cutter. Bake on greased cookie sheets in a 350° oven for 10 minutes. Makes about 6 dozen.

LILLIAN KING'S LITTLE NUT CAKES

One pint of sugar — to which add four unbeaten eggs and cream. Then one pint flour and one pint of hickory nuts meats mixed and added. One spoonful cinnamon, and grated nutmeg, mixed half and half. No milk, no butter. Nothing to raise them but the eggs. Butter long pan and drop on far apart. One teaspoon full for each cake. They bake very quickly and spread the right size. Buy nuts all picked out at confectioners.

Substitute 2 teaspoons cinnamon for 1 spoonful, and 1 tablespoon nutmeg for the grated nutmeg. Chopped walnuts or pecans may be used in place of hickory nuts.

Sift flour with cinnamon and nutmeg. Set aside. Cream the sugar and eggs together until mixture is thick and creamy. Add dry ingredients to the creamed mixture and work until thoroughly blended. Work in the nuts. Drop by heaping teaspoons onto buttered cookie sheets. Bake in a 350° oven for 10 to 12 minutes. Makes 8 dozen.

MRS. ARNOLD'S DROP CAKES

1 pound flour, ¾ pound sugar, ½ pound butter, 4 eggs, one glass rosewater, cinnamon and nutmeg. Beat the materials well. Drop them from a spoon on to tin sheets. Bake from 20 to 30 minutes.

1-½ cups sugar	2 tablespoons rosewater
½ cup butter or margarine	1 teaspoon cinnamon
2 eggs	1 teaspoon nutmeg
2 cups flour	

Sift flour with cinnamon and nutmeg. Set aside. Cream the butter or margarine and gradually add sugar. Continue creaming until mixture is fluffy. Beat in eggs, one at a time. Add sifted flour mixture to the creamed mixture alternately with rosewater. Drop by rounded teaspoonfuls onto greased cookie sheets. Bake in a 350° oven for 10 minutes. Cool on racks before removing from sheets. Makes about 3-½ dozen.

Rosewater may be obtained from a drugstore. Just ask the pharmacist. In absence of rosewater, use 1 teaspoon vanilla and slightly less than 2 tablespoons water.

COCONUT JUMBLES

Two eggs, 3 teacups white sugar, one teacup butter, one teacup sour cream, one scant teaspoonful soda, five teacups flour, one large coconut grated. Roll in sugar and drop on the pans. Add nuts last.

1 egg	½ teaspoon baking soda
1-½ cups sugar	2 cups flaked or grated
½ cup butter or margarine	coconut
½ cup sour milk	½ cup chopped nuts
2-½ cups flour	

Beat egg until frothy. Add sugar, then soft butter or margarine, beating well after each addition. Add sour milk and mix thoroughly. Sift flour and soda together and add. Add coconut and nuts last. Chill dough one hour. When ready to bake, grease hands and form dough into small balls. Roll in white sugar and place on greased cookie sheets. Bake in a 350° oven for 10 to 12 minutes. Makes about 4 dozen.

LEMON JUMBLES

One pound sugar, ¾ pound butter, 4 eggs, the juice and rind of one lemon and as little flour as will enable you to make into small cakes with your hands.

2-½ to 3 cups flour
1 teaspoon baking soda
¼ teaspoon salt
¾ cup butter or margarine

2 cups sugar
3 eggs
juice and grated rind of
1 lemon

Sift dry ingredients together. Set aside. Cream butter or margarine with sugar until creamy and light. Add eggs, lemon juice and grated rind. Add enough of the sifted flour mixture to make a smooth, workable dough. Drop from a tablespoon onto buttered cookie sheets and bake in a 350° oven for 10 to 12 minutes or until done. Makes 3 to 4 dozen.

MRS. T. C. REYNOLDS' COOKIES

1 cup W.I. molasses (never sorghum)
2 cups sugar
1 heaping cup lard or butter
a pinch of salt
½ cup water
2 heaping teaspoonfuls of ground cloves or spice to taste
1 large tablespoon soda in molasses
Flour enough to roll on very thin
Bake in moderate oven. Grease baking pans.

In this deliciously flavored spice cookie, we made no substitutions — just a few clarifications. Use 1-¼ cups of butter or margarine, ¼ teaspoon salt, 7 cups of sifted flour, and 4 teaspoons of baking soda.

Cream the butter or margarine with sugar until fluffy. Add water, spice and salt, and mix well. Blend in molasses and baking soda mixture. Add flour and mix thoroughly. Turn batter out onto a well floured board. Roll dough thin and cut with a cookie cutter. The dough you will find quite sticky. Place on buttered cookie sheets and bake in a 375° oven for 10 minutes. Makes about 9 dozen large cookies.

ALMOND WAFERS

Cream ½ cup butter. Add gradually 1 cup powdered sugar, then drop by drop ½ cup milk and last two cups pastry flour and ½ teaspoon of vanilla. Spread very thin on the bottom of an <u>inverted</u> dripping pan buttered. Mark in squares. Sprinkle with almonds blanched and chopped fine and bake in a moderate oven about 5 minutes. Separate the wafers with a pointed knife. Lift one by one, turn, and roll one corner or side on the hot pan.

Cream the butter and gradually add sugar until mixture is fluffy. Sift flour and add to creamed mixture alternately with milk. Add vanilla and blend thoroughly. Butter an 11 by 10-inch cookie sheet. Butter hands and pat dough out thin. Mark in 2-inch squares and sprinkle with ½ cup almonds that have been chopped in a blender. Bake in a 350° oven for 15 minutes or until lightly browned. Makes 2 dozen. These cookies tend to break when rolled, but are very pretty left in squares, and are quite delicious.

Acquisition by an army wife of a new stove or range was cause for great celebration. When Marian Sloan Russell was able to obtain her first step stove in 1866, she stated that "it was the light of my eyes and the joy of my heart." Her new stove had two steps and each step could be used for cooking. "That stove was the envy of all my neighbors," she wrote, "and one woman offered me $50.00 for it." Marian, of course did not sell her new stove, and it was still one of her prized possessions when she and her husband settled permanently in Stonewall, Colorado.

TO TELL GOOD EGGS — Put in water and if the buts turn up they are not fresh.

CAKES

Because of the lack of variety in their meat and vegetable dishes, army wives depended on desserts to add flavor and distinction to their meals. Of all desserts, the 19th century homemaker's pride was her cakes. Cakes were associated with entertaining and there were special cakes for sad as well as joyous occasions. There were Christmas cakes, Valentine's Day cakes, election cakes, and even funeral cakes.

Cake baking 100 years ago was considered an art, and actual baking of the cake was judged to be more critical than mixing of the ingredients. A uniform oven temperature was vital for the cake to rise properly, and this was usually easier said than done. According to an old training book for army bakers and cooks, the only practical way to determine temperature of an oven was "to insert the hand well into it and count the number of seconds you were able to keep it there. The burning sensation experienced about the roots of the nails is sufficiently uniform in those performing the duty of a cook to render this a reliable method, and it should be followed by the experienced chef as well as by the student cook." With such a "reliable method" one can readily understand why baking was considered such a precarious undertaking.

Mrs. Grierson's cookbook contains numerous cake recipes, but very few frosting recipes. It is true that many cakes of the 19th century were not frosted, but because Mrs. Grierson mentioned which icings were used in some of her cake recipes, we were a little disappointed not to find more.

churn

APPLE FRUIT CAKE

2 cups dried apples soaked over night, chopped fine, and cooked in 2 cups of molasses. When cold add 2 cups sugar, 1 cup butter, 5 cups flour, 3 eggs, 1 cup milk, 1 teaspoonful soda, spice of all kinds.

We changed the procedure, but did not alter the ingredients except to designate amounts of the various spices we used. Cover dried apples with cold water. Place over heat and simmer for 30 minutes or until apples are tender. Drain well and set aside. Sift flour with baking soda and:

2 teaspoons cinnamon	2 teaspoons allspice
2 teaspoons nutmeg	1 teaspoon ground cloves
1 teaspoon mace	

Set aside sifted ingredients. Cream the butter and sugar until light. Add eggs, one at a time, and beat well. Add sifted dry ingredients to the creamed mixture alternately with milk. Blend in apples and molasses. Turn batter into a greased 10-inch tube pan or Bundt pan and bake in a 300° oven for about 2 hours or until cake tests done. This spicy, sweet cake tastes very much like old-fashioned gingerbread.

MRS. CATTIN'S SPONGE CAKE

5 eggs beaten separately, one tumbler of sugar. Fill a tumbler half full of flour, then fill heaping full of flour after adding a scant spoon of baking powder to the half tumbler. Beat the yolks and sugar and rind and piece of ½ lemon. Then add flour and whites. Makes two small loaves. Bake about ½ hour. Also nice in layers with chocolate between.

5 eggs, separated	¼ cup water
1-½ cups sugar	1-½ cups flour
½ lemon, rind and juice	1 teaspoon baking powder
½ teaspoon salt	

Beat egg yolks. Add sugar, lemon rind and juice, salt, and water and mix. Sift flour and baking powder together and add to egg mixture. Beat egg whites until stiff. Fold into batter. Turn batter into 2 ungreased loaf pans and bake in a 325° oven for 30 minutes or until cakes test done.

DOLLY VARDEN

Many "old time" cakes were named for famous people. There were cakes named for, among others, Martha Washington, Henry Clay, and Robert E. Lee. Some were even named for fictional characters. The following recipe takes its name from Dolly Varden, the delightful character in Dickens' *Barnaby Rudge*. Dolly's popularity encouraged fashions as well as food to be named for her. In the 1870's the "Dolly Varden" dress and hat emerged, as well as this delicious cake.

THE DOLLY VARDEN CAKE

2 *coffee cups of sugar*	3-1/2 *coffee cups of flour*
1 *coffee cup of butter*	4 *eggs*
3/4 *coffee cup of milk*	2 *spoons of baking powder*

Divide in three parts. To one third add one teaspoon of ground cloves, cinnamon, a little nutmeg, and currants, raisins, and citron to taste. Bake in three common long head pans each third separately, two thirds being white, one black. When done, put together with jelly and frosting, in three layers like a jelly cake. It is very pretty when sliced across the loaf, the dark part forming the middle layer. I flavor all with any extract I wish before I divide it.

2 cups sugar	1 cup butter or margarine
1 cup milk	3-1/2 cups flour, sifted
4 eggs, separated	3 teaspoons baking powder
1/4 teaspoon salt	1 teaspoon vanilla

Cream butter and sugar. Beat in egg yolks, one at a time. Sift flour with baking powder and salt, and add to creamed mixture alternately with milk, beginning and ending with the flour mixture. Add vanilla and fold in stiffly beaten egg whites. Divide batter into three equal parts and to one add:

1/2 teaspoon ground cloves	1/2 cup raisins or currants
1 teaspoon cinnamon	1/4 cup candied citron, if desired
1/4 teaspoon nutmeg	

Pour into 3 greased and floured layer pans. Bake at 350° for 20 minutes or until cakes test done. Remove from pans and cool. Put layers together with jelly; spice layer in the middle. Frost with a butter cream frosting.

MRS. VOGEL'S WHITE CAKE

2 cups of sugar
¾ cup of butter
1-¼ cup of milk
4 cups of flour
Whites of six eggs
2 rounding spoons of baking powder

Cream the butter and sugar.
Add the milk and 3 cups of flour and half the whites, very stiff. Then add the 4th cup of flour and the baking powder and the remaining 3 whites. Bake in a sheet at least 2 inches tall and frost with plain or chocolate frosting. Delicious.

We followed original instructions, beating egg whites until they were very stiff before adding them to the creamed mixture. We used 2 teaspoons baking powder instead of "2 rounding spoons" and baked the cake in a greased and floured 9 by 13-inch pan at 350° for approximately 30 minutes.

PLUM CAKE
(Fine)

One cup of butter
2 cups of sugar
½ cup of milk
½ cup of molasses
Yolks of 3 eggs, whites of 2
½ teaspoon soda
½ teaspoon cream of tartar
4 cups of flour

½ pound stoned raisins
½ pound currants
Citron
2 tablespoons mixed spices
¼ cake chocolate, melted
Small wine glass of brandy or fruit juice

1 cup butter
  (softened, not melted)
2 cups sugar
½ cup milk
½ cup molasses
3 eggs, separated
½ pound raisins
½ pound currants
¼ pound chopped citron

4 cups flour
3 teaspoons cinnamon
2 teaspoons allspice
1 teaspoon nutmeg
½ teaspoon cream of tartar
½ teaspoon baking soda
1 square chocolate, melted
½ cup brandy

Sift flour with spices, soda, and cream of tartar. Cream butter and sugar. Add egg yolks one at a time, beating after each addition. Add liquids (molasses, milk, and melted chocolate) alternately with flour mixture. Beat egg whites until stiff but not dry and fold into batter. Stir in brandy, raisins, currants, and citron. Bake at 300° about 2-½ to 3 hours in a 12-cup "Teflon" coated Bundt pan. (Cake may be baked in large tube pan or 2 loaf pans. Grease bottom and sides of pans and line with wax paper.) Place pan of water on bottom rack in oven to prevent cake from browning too quickly.

FRENCH LOAF CAKE

5 cups powdered sugar, 3 cups fresh butter, 2 cups milk, 6 eggs, 10 cups flour, wine glass wine, same of brandy, 3 nutmegs, 1 teaspoonful of soda, 1 pound of raisins, ½ pound citron.

The original recipe makes five cakes. We reduced the proportions to make one 9 by 5 by 3-inch loaf.

1 cup powdered sugar	½ cup butter
⅓ cup milk	2 eggs
2 cups flour, sifted	½ teaspoon nutmeg
1 teaspoon baking soda	½ cup raisins
2 tablespoons red wine	¼ cup citrons, diced
2 tablespoons brandy	

Sift flour, baking soda, and nutmeg together and set aside. Cream the butter, gradually adding sugar and beating until light and fluffy. Beat in eggs, one at a time. Add flour mixture to the creamed mixture alternately with milk, wine, and brandy, beginning and ending with the dry ingredients. Stir in raisins and citron. Turn batter into a greased and floured loaf pan and bake at 350° for 50 minutes or until cake tests done.

Dutch oven

COFFEE CAKE

2 eggs, 2 cups of sugar, ¾ butter, a cup strong coffee, one table-
spoon cinnamon, cloves and nutmeg, 2 tablespoons brandy, one
teaspoon soda, two of cream of tarter, 1 pound raisins, ¼ pound
citron, 3-½ cups flour. Extra flour for fruit.

Add ¼ cup flour to this recipe and stir it through raisins and citron until they are coated thoroughly. Sift together the remaining flour, baking soda, cream of tartar, cinnamon, cloves, and nutmeg, and set aside. Cream the butter and gradually add sugar until the mixture is smooth. Beat in eggs, one at a time. Stir flour mixture into creamed mixture alternately with coffee and brandy. Fold in the fruit. Turn batter into a greased and floured 9 by 13-inch pan. Bake at 350° for 45 to 50 minutes or until cake tests done. Unusually large amounts of cinnamon, nutmeg, and cloves make this a delicious, rich-flavored spice cake.

MARBLE CAKE

Mrs. Choate, Woburn, Massachusetts

1-½ cups butter, 2 cups sugar, 5 eggs, ½ cup sweet milk, 4 cups
flour, 1 teaspoon cream tartar, ½ teaspoon soda, essence of lemon.
Rub butter and sugar to a cream. Beat whites and yolks separately.
Add yolks first to butter and sugar, then whites, half the flour,
with cream tartar mixed well. Then the milk with the soda, the
rest of the flour. Divide the dough. To one half add a half tea-
cupful of dark West India Molasses with a large teaspoonful of
cloves, the same of cinnamon stirred into it. A large coffee cupful
of stoned raisons, with a tablespoonful of flour stirred into them.
Drop alternately spoonfuls of dark and light batter.

We made no changes in the ingredients except to use ½ teaspoon lemon extract for "essence of lemon," ⅓ cup molasses, and 1 cup seedless raisins.

Cream the butter. Add sugar gradually, beating until light and fluffy. Add egg yolks and lemon extract. Sift together flour, cream of tartar, and baking soda and add to the creamed mixture alternately with milk, beating until smooth. Beat egg whites until stiff and fold into the mixture. Divide batter in half. To one half add cloves and cinnamon alernately with molasses. Work in raisins last. Alternate layers or large spoonfuls of dark and light batter into a greased and lightly floured 9 by 15-inch pan. Cut through with a knife to improve marbling. Bake in 350° oven for about 45 minutes or until cake tests done. A chocolate frosting topped with nuts makes this a "mighty fine" cake.

MOTHER'S CUP CAKES

1 cup of butter, 2 cups sugar, 4 cups flour, 1 cup milk, 3 eggs, soda and nutmeg.
This can be used for jelly cake.
Makes cookies the same without the milk. Add ginger if you please.

1 cup butter or margarine	1 cup sour milk
2 cups sugar	3 eggs
4 cups flour, sifted	1 teaspoon baking soda
½ teaspoon nutmeg	

Cream the butter or margarine. Gradually add sugar and continue creaming until fluffy. Sift together flour and nutmeg and set aside. Mix baking soda with sour milk. Add eggs, one at a time to the creamed butter and sugar mixture, beating well after each addition. Add flour mixture to creamed mixture alternately with sour milk mixture. Turn batter into greased or paper-lined muffin tins, filling no more than half full. Bake in 350° oven for about 25 minutes. **Makes 30 cupcakes.**

Cookies made from this recipe, by just omitting the milk, were quite like the tasty old-fashioned tea cakes. We also made another batch of cookies substituting 2-½ teaspoons baking powder for baking soda. These cookies were fairly crisp and when sprinkled with powdered sugar were also quite good. Makes 6 dozen.

CLOSING CRACKS IN CAST-IRON STOVES—Good wood ashes are to be shifted through a fine sieve, to which is to be added the same quantity of clay finely pulverized, together with a little salt. This mixture is to be moistened with water enough to make a paste, and the crack of the stove filled with it. The cement does not peel off or breakaway, and assumes an extreme degree of hardness after being heated. The stove must be cool when the application is made. The same substance may be used in setting the plates of a stove or fitting stove pipes, serving to render all the joints perfectly tight.

JENNY LIND

The following cake was named for Jenny Lind, the greatest soprano of the mid-eighteen hundreds. The "Swedish Nightingale," as she was fondly called, made only one U.S. tour, 1850-1852. For anyone who had the privilege of seeing her, it was a rare and thrilling occasion. In 1851, Benjamin Grierson, his sister Mary, his brother John, and John's wife Elizabeth all shared this experience. The following is taken from a letter written by Mary Grierson to her future sister-in-law Alice Kirk, describing the events that surrounded her journey from Jacksonville to St. Louis to hear Jenny Lind:

"Oh! I must not forget the joy of my life. I have heard—have seen—Jenny—living—breathing—singing, Jenny Lind. I must say only what all say that she is above all description. She must be heard. Could I have known what I would have lost by not hearing her, it would have been a life-long sorrow, but I have heard her. I could talk of her for hours, but I cannot write. When she came to St. Louis, Ben went down to hear her. I thought it right. But the high price of the tickets compelled me to decide that I ought not to think of such an indulgence for myself. John was there on business — went to the first concert — came home with such descriptions of her music and such an urgent request for me to come that Elizabeth, Mr. Howard and I set off. I shall always be glad that I have heard her. Indeed I would have considered myself paid — for expense and trouble — in listening to one solo on the voiloncello played by a young man — one of the orchestra. Oh! I wish you could have heard it. Our seats cost us $6.50 each — besides the expense of going and coming and our expenses there. The poor I know ought not to expect to indulge themselves as the rich can, but we cannot estimate Jenny Lind's singing in dollars and cents. They are nothing. She gave five concerts in St. Louis. Ben heard them all."

THE JENNY LIND CAKE

2 eggs
2 cups of sugar
½ cup of butter
1 cup of sweet cream or milk

3-½ cups flour
3 teaspoonfuls baking powder
Flavor to taste, rind of the
lemon, if thought best, salt

Cream for the inside

2 apples, grated
1 cup of white sugar
1 egg. Cook until it boils up, then add the juice of one lemon.
To be baked like Jelly Cake and spread with the cream.

2 cups sugar

½ cup butter, margarine, or lard

2 eggs, large

1 cup sweet cream or milk

3-½ cups flour

3 teaspoons baking powder

1 teaspoon salt

1 teaspoon vanilla or 2 teaspoons
lemon or orange peel, grated

Cream the sugar with shortening until light. Add eggs and beat well. Stir in milk and flavoring. Sift flour, salt, and baking powder together and add to the creamed mixture. Blend until batter is smooth. Turn batter into two 9-inch layer pans that have been greased and floured. Bake at 350° for about 35 minutes or until cakes test done.

Cream Filling

2 apples, grated or 1-½ cups applesauce

1 egg (plus 1 tablespoon cornstarch if you do use applesauce and it is thin)

1 cup white sugar

2 to 3 tablespoons lemon juice or 1 to 2 tablespoons lemonade concentrate

Bring apples (or applesauce), beaten egg, and sugar to a boil. Remove from heat and add lemon juice or lemonade concentrate. When cakes are cool, split the layers. Place first layer of cake on the plate and alternate layers of cake and filling until both are used up.

Egg beater

JULIA BUCKMASTER'S SPICE CAKE

Cream ½ cup butter—add to this ¼ cup dry cocoa, working well together. Beat the yolks of 3 eggs well and add to the cocoa and butter. Put into a sieve 1 cup of flour and 3 teaspoons baking powder. Sift together. Ready to mix with the cake. Mix 1 teaspoon cinnamon, ¼ teaspoon cloves with one cup fine granulated sugar, or you may use vanilla instead of cloves. Add sugar and spice to butter and beat well. Add whites of eggs alternately with flour and ½ cup cold water. Bake in tin pans.

We baked this in a 9-inch square pan at 350° for 25 to 30 minutes, making no changes in ingredients or procedure. A creamy white icing made this exceptionally light spice cake one of our favorites.

WASHINGTON PIE OR BOSTON CREAM CAKE
Mrs. Barr's

2 cups of sugar, ¾ of a cup of butter, 1 cup of milk, 4 cups of flour, 4 eggs, 2 teaspoons baking powder, flavor with vanilla, bake in 4 layers—2 in a loaf. For Filling: 1-½ pints of sweet milk, 3 tablespoons of flour, yolks of two or three eggs, sweeten to taste, small lump of butter, flavor with vanilla. After putting together make a meringue of the whites of 5 eggs, with sugar enough to keep from falling; spread over the cakes, and return to the oven to brown lightly.

Today we make a definite distinction between a Washington Pie and a Boston Cream Cake. The pie usually has a jam or jelly filling, while the cake has custard or cream between the layers. Now both are generally topped with powdered sugar or some type of glaze. We prefer the powdered sugar topping, but find the meringue used in the original recipe to be different as well as quite tasty.

2 cups sugar	¾ cup butter
1 cup milk	3 cups flour
4 eggs	2 teaspoons baking powder
½ teaspoon vanilla	½ teaspoon salt

Sift flour, baking powder, and salt, and set aside. Cream the butter and gradually beat in sugar and vanilla. Beat eggs until light and add to creamed mixture. Then add flour mixture alternately with milk, and blend until batter is smooth. Turn batter into 3 8-inch round layer pans that have been greased and floured. Bake in a 350° oven for 25 to 30 minutes, or until cake tests done. Cool completely before filling.

Filling:

1-½ pints milk ½ cup sugar
Yolks of 3 eggs ½ teaspoon salt
1 tablespoon butter ½ teaspoon vanilla
3 tablespoons flour

Mix sugar, flour, and salt in saucepan. Add ½ cup milk and stir until smooth. Pour in remaining milk and cook over low heat until thickened. Add mixture to beaten egg yolks; return to saucepan and cook for 2 minutes longer. Add vanilla, and cool. Put layers together with the cream filling.

Meringue:

Whites of 5 eggs
10 tablespoons sugar
1 teaspoon vanilla

Beat egg whites until stiff; add sugar two tablespoons at a time, beating well after each addition. Add flavoring. Spread over top and sides of cake and brown in a 350° oven for about 15 minutes until lightly browned.

CAKE WITHOUT EGGS — No. 1

2 cups and a half of flour, one cup of sugar, one cup sweet milk, one half cup of butter, one teaspoonful of cream of tartar, one half of soda. Flavor with lemon.

Mrs. Grierson had several recipes for cakes without eggs. To distinguish them from one another she gave them numbers. Whether or not the numbers also denoted quality is hard to tell, but this recipe for a cake without eggs, possessing the number one, was best in the group of recipes tested.

Cream butter and sugar until the mixture is light and fluffy. Stir in ½ teaspoon lemon extract. Sift dry ingredients together and add to the creamed mixture alternately with milk. Begin and end with the dry ingredients. Turn batter into a greased and floured 9-inch square pan and bake in a 350° oven for 25 minutes or until cake tests done.

SCRIPTURE CAKE

1 cup of butter	*Judges 5, verse 25*
3 cups of sugar	*Jeremiah 6, verse 20*
3-½ cups of flour	*I Kings 4, verse 22*
2 cups of raisins	*I Samuel 30, verse 12*
2 cups of figs	*I Samuel 30, verse 12*
1 cup of water	*Genesis 24, verse 17*
1 cup of almonds	*Genesis 24, verse 17*
6 eggs	*Isaiah 10, verse 14*
One tablespoon of honey	*Exodus 16, verse 21*
A pinch of salt	*Leviticus 2, verse 31*
Spices to taste	

Follow Solomon's advice for making good boys, and you will have a good cake.   *Proverbs 13, verse 24*

A form for Scripture Cake sent to "Household News" by a woman who realized $100 for the sale of slices of this cake with its receipt for two days at a church fair.

1 cup butter	1 cup slivered almonds
3 cups sugar	1 tablespoon honey
3-½ cups flour	⅛ teaspoon salt
6 eggs	1 teaspoon cinnamon
2 cups raisins	1 teaspoon allspice
2 cups chopped dried figs	¼ teaspoon cloves
1 cup water	

Mix raisins and figs with ¼ cup flour; set aside. Sift remaining flour with salt and spices. Cream butter until light. Add sugar gradually. Continue beating until mixture is very fluffy. Add eggs, one at a time, beating at least one minute after each addition. Add water and honey alternately with flour mixture. Stir in almonds, figs, raisins. Bake at 300° 2-½ to 3 hours in a 12-cup "Teflon" coated Bundt pan. (Cake may be baked in large tube pan or 2 loaf pans. Grease bottom and sides of pans and line with wax paper.) Place pan of water on bottom rack in oven to prevent cake from browning too quickly.

PIES

Pie is as traditional a food in the United States as roast beef and mashed potatoes. Originally the word pie referred to a deep-dish meat recipe having a thick crust, but by the 19th century the word more often than not meant a dessert baked in a shallow pan. As today, the cook of the eighteen hundreds probably baked more apple pies than any other. Apples by the bushel were peeled, quartered, and hung on strings to dry so that apple pies could be made all through the winter. We have included in this section one of Mrs. Grierson's recipes using dried apples. It is not only fun to make, but will get many a compliment from those who are lucky enough to taste it.

Sometimes army wives would be so homesick for certain products they would pay exorbitant prices to obtain them. Mollie McIntosh, wife of Lieutenant Donald McIntosh, Seventh Cavalry, stated that in an "orgy of extravagance" she paid $1.50 for a dozen bananas in 1875, in Bismarck. She also remembered paying $25.00 for a barrel of apples to be shipped in the fall from Oregon by oxcart to her at Fort Lincoln, Dakota Territory, and when they arrived every one was frozen! While Elizabeth Burt was at Fort C. F. Smith, in 1866, a new post baker arrived. Being a rather enterprising fellow, he brought with him a barrel of dried blackberries, and with the help of his wife, he made blackberry pies which he promptly sold to the soldiers for seventy-five cents each. Every western army wife sometime in her "career" undoubtedly paid a very high price for some favorite pie or pie making ingredient.

Despite the many recipes in Mrs. Grierson's cookbook for pie fillings, there is no basic pie crust recipe. Similar to today's crust, pie shells were usually made with ice water, fresh butter or sweet lard, salt, and flour. Probably the making of a pastry shell was thought to be so basic that no written instructions were needed. There is also not a great deal of variety among Mrs. Grierson's pie filling recipes. For example, there are thirteen lemon pie recipes of which we have used only two. As a result this section may appear a bit skimpy.

PINKIE PLATT'S APPLE PIE RECEIPT

*1 quart dried apple sauce, sifted through the collander, yolks of
3 eggs, beaten with 1 cup of sugar, then add 1 cup milk, then
apples. Put into a crust. Beat whites to a stiff froth with 2
tablespoons sugar and* <u>*return*</u> *to the oven to brown.*

9-inch unbaked pie shell	2 egg yolks
2 cups dried apples (8-oz. bag)	½ cup sugar
4 cups boiling water	½ cup milk
¼ teaspoon salt	1 teaspoon cinnamon or allspice

Wash apples and place in boiling water with salt. Make sure
apples are completely covered by water. Reduce heat and simmer
for 15-20 minutes. Remove from heat and drain in a collander.
Set aside. Beat egg yolks and add sugar and spice. Mix thoroughly.
Add milk and blend well. Stir in apples last. Pour mixture into
unbaked pie shell and bake in a 425° oven for 30 minutes.

<u>For Meringue:</u>

2 egg whites	½ teaspon vanilla <u>or</u>
¼ teaspoon cream of tartar	¼ teaspoon almond or other
6 tablespoons sugar	flavoring
¼ teaspoon salt	

Place egg whites in a bowl. Add cream of tartar, salt, and flavoring. Beat with electric mixer until mixture is foamy. Add sugar,
2 tablespoons at a time, beating well after each addition. Continue beating until meringue is smooth. Spread on hot or slightly
cooled filling. Brown in 350° oven for 12-15 minutes.

apples

LEMON PIE

The following is taken from a newspaper clipping found in the original cookbook: "EXCELLENT LEMON PIES — As usually made, lemon pies, however palatable, are indigestible and not to be recommended. The pieces of lemon rind in them are as bad for the stomach as so many gravel stones. The following directions furnished for the American Agriculturist, have been several times tried, and we find the pies both digestible and delicious: For two pies, take two lemons, grate away the outer yellow coating and chop the rest very fine. Into two teacupfuls of hot water, stir well two tablespoonfuls of corn starch, and boil; add two teacupfuls of white sugar; when cool, add the beaten yolks of four eggs; then add the chopped lemons with their juice, stirring the whole well together. Line two tin or earthen-ware pie plates with pie crust, pour in the material and bake until the crust is done. Beat the whites of the four eggs to a froth, adding five or six tablespoonfuls of white sugar, and pour over the pies while hot; return them to the oven, and bake to a delicate brown. We have never eaten anything of the pie kind superior to the above preparation."

We found that this recipe makes only enough filling for one 9-inch pie. It is quite good and easy to prepare. We made only a few alterations to the original recipe, but have re-written the text for clarification.

One 9-inch pie shell, unbaked	1-3/4 cups hot water
2 lemons	2 cups sugar
2 tablespoons cornstarch	4 egg yolks
1/4 cup cold water	

Grate outer yellow rind of lemons. Peel off the white undercoat and discard. Chop remaining lemons very fine. Set aside. Stir cornstarch into cold water, mixing thoroughly. Add hot water and bring mixture to a boil, stirring constantly. Add sugar and continue stirring until it dissolves. Remove from heat and cool. Beat yolks of eggs and add to cooled mixture. Add grated rinds and chopped lemons with their juice. Blend well. Pour mixture into an unbaked pie shell and bake in a 425° oven for about 15 minutes, or until crust is done.

For Meringue:

4 egg whites	1/4 teaspoon salt
1/4 teaspoon cream of tartar	1/2 teaspoon vanilla extract
5 or 6 tablespoons sugar	

Follow instructions for Meringue as found with Apple Pie, and brown as directed.

SISTER FANNIE'S CREAM PIE

2 pints milk (skimmed will do), 1-½ tea cups sugar, yolks of 3 eggs and white of one, two heaping tablespoonfuls flour. Beat the yolks and flour and sugar and one white together. Let the milk get boiling hot then pour in the beaten parts and stir till thick. Make your crust and bake it. Fill your plates. Then beat the two remaining whites and spread over the top. Return to the oven to brown. A little butter, a little salt, and something for flavoring. Vanilla is best.

9-inch baked pastry shell	½ teaspoon salt
2 cups milk	1 heaping tablespoon flour
1 egg plus 1 egg yolk	1 teaspoon vanilla

Beat egg and egg yolk with sugar, vanilla, and flour. Bring milk to a boil, then remove from the heat. Add egg mixture to milk, and blend well. Cook mixture over medium heat until it thickens and boils. Pour hot mixture into a baked pastry shell. Top with meringue or nutmeg or serve plain. Follow instructions for Meringue as found with the Apple Pie, but in this instance use 3 eggs instead of 2. Allow pie to cool and set at room temperature before cutting. This is absolutely delicious. It tastes like a delicately flavored, slightly fluffy, custard.

RAISIN PIE

Two cups of raisins. Wash and set on to boil in enough water to cover them. Make a pretty rich paste to cover your plates. When the raisins are nicely swelled, dredge among them two tablespoonfuls flour to thicken the water. Add sugar. Spread on the paste and bake in a moderate oven. Make a whip of three eggs, two tablespoons sugar. When the pies are cool, spread the whip over them. If you like put a few swelled raisins on top. Set in a cool oven to set.

Pastry for a 1-crust 9-inch pie	½ cup sugar
2 cups raisins	2 tablespoons flour
2 cups boiling water	

Cook raisins in boiling water until tender, about 5 minutes. Stir in sugar and flour. Bring to a boil; reduce heat and simmer, stirring, until mixture is thick and smooth. This will take only a few minutes. Cool and pour into an unbaked pie shell and bake in a 425° oven for 30-35 minutes.

For Meringue:

3 egg whites	6 tablespoons sugar
¼ teaspoon cream of tartar	¼ teaspoon salt
½ teaspoon vanilla or ¼ teaspoon almond or other flavoring	

Follow directions for Meringue as found with Apple Pie. For those who like raisins, this is a delightful treat.

TO RESTORE SOUR MILK OR CREAM—Milk or cream, when it has turned sour, may be restored to its original sweetness by means of a small quantity of carbonate or magnesia. When the acidity is slight, half a teaspoon of the powder to a pint of milk.

MISS SHEPARD'S ENGLISH CURD PIE
100 Years Old

Set a quart of new milk upon the fire with 2 or 3 blades of mace, and when ready to boil add to it the yolks and whites of 9 eggs well beaten and as much salt as will lie on a small knife point. Let it boil until the whey is clear, then drain it in a cloth or hair sieve. Season with sugar and a little cinnamon, rose water, orange flower water or white wine to your taste and put into a star form or any other. Let it stand several hours before you turn it into a dish and put round it a thick cream or a custard.

2 cups sour milk	¼ teaspoon ground mace
4 eggs	2 tablespoons rose water
¼ teaspoon salt	2 tablespoons orange water or
3 tablespoons sugar	white wine
¼ teaspoon ground cinnamon	

This delicious custard-like dessert is very easy to make. We followed the original directions, making substitutions for ingredients where necessary, and draining the boiled mixture through cheese cloth. If you like a little sweeter dessert, add an additional tablespoon of sugar. Top with whipped cream or pour a custard over it.

ANOTHER "LEMON PUDDING"

From Mother's Old Book

Boil a pint of cream and a pint of milk, or a quart of new milk. Pour it over a pounded cracker. Grate in a nutmeg, rind and juice of 2 lemons. 1 glass of wine, rose water, ¼ pound butter, sugar to taste. Beat 8 eggs and add last. Cover the dish with a fluff-paste, or pour in the mixture. Bake one half hour.

The original recipe makes filling for two large pies. We made half the recipe and it was perfect for one 9-inch crust.

9-inch pie shell, unbaked
1 cup light cream or evaporated milk
1 cup milk
½ cracker (2 squares)
2 teaspoons nutmeg

1 lemon, juice and grated rind
¼ cup white wine
2 tablespoons rosewater
4 tablespoons butter or margarine
1 cup sugar
4 eggs

Pound cracker and place in large mixing bowl. Boil canned evaporated milk or cream with the milk, and pour it over cracker crumbs. Add grated rind and juice of lemon, nutmeg, wine, rosewater, butter, and sugar. Mix thoroughly. Beat eggs separately and add. Blend thoroughly. Pour mixture into pie shell and bake in a 450° oven for 10 minutes, then reduce heat to 350° and bake another 30 minutes. This is more like a custard pie than a traditional lemon pie. We found it not only slightly unusual, but very tasty.

SQUASH PIE

Mrs. King, Jacksonville, Illinois

One pint squash—steamed and sifted, one pint milk, 1 cup white sugar, three eggs well beaten. Better to beat separately and add whites last. One half nutmeg, one teaspoon vanilla. Mix well together and pour over the last thing. Salt to taste. Milk cold.

9-inch pie shell, unbaked
2 cups frozen squash, thawed
2 cups milk
1 cup sugar

3 eggs, separated
½ teaspoon nutmeg
¼ teaspoon salt
1 teaspoon vanilla

We did not alter this recipe except to use frozen squash. Mix all ingredients except egg whites in saucepan and bring to a boil, stirring to prevent sticking. Beat egg whites until stiff and fold into squash mixture. Pour into pie shell and bake at 450° for 10 minutes. Reduce heat to 325° and continue to bake for 45 more minutes.

MOLASSES PIE

The yolks of 4 eggs, beaten light, one large tablespoonful flour, one pint molasses, two tablespoonfuls of strong vinegar, two tablespoonfuls ginger. Bake, then add the whites of the eggs, well beaten, with three spoonfuls sugar. Return to the oven to brown.

9-inch pie shell, unbaked
4 eggs, separated
2 tablespoons flour
2 teaspoons ground ginger

2 tablespoons vinegar
2 cups molasses
3 tablespoons sugar

Beat egg yolks until light. Add flour, ginger, and vinegar and blend thoroughly. Mix in molasses. Pour into pie shell and bake in a 350° oven for 40-45 minutes. A meringue may be made from the egg whites and sugar, spread on the hot pie and browned in a 425° oven for 5 minutes or until top is lightly colored.

It was the consensus of all who tested this pie that meringue was not the right topping for today's taste. Whipped cream, whipped topping, or a small scoop of vanilla ice cream would be more suitable. Our "samplers" also offered various opinions as to what the pie tasted like. Many thought it tasted like mincement, raisin, or pumpkin pie. We felt the reason for this was that very few people today have acquired a taste for molasses.

PUDDINGS
AND OTHER DESSERTS

It was not until recent times that quick cooking and instant puddings began to replace traditional boiled and baked puddings. Alice Grierson's cookbook, like many cookbooks of its time, contains many dessert pudding and pudding sauce recipes. Dessert puddings are relatively modern. Only when sugar began to replace molasses and honey as a sweetening agent in the early 19th century did sweet puddings begin to gain in popularity over traditional steak and kidney puddings.

With boiled puddings, it was generally the rule to serve a cold sauce made of sugar, eggs, butter, flavoring, and brandy. Baked puddings were usually topped with a rich boiled sauce, whipped cream or ice cream. We have included in this section the most delicious of the dessert recipes tested. All are highly recommended and well worth the extra preparation time.

Fruit puddings could be made only when fruit was in season or when an army wife was lucky enough to obtain dried or canned fruits. When Marian Sloan Russell and her husband, Lieutenant Richard C. Russell, were stationed at Camp Nichols, Indian Territory in 1865, they paid $2.00 for one small can of peaches. The peaches, along with their other supplies, had been brought by freight wagon from Fort Union, some 130 miles away. If a frontier woman had to pay such high prices for canned peaches, it is probable the following dessert was not made as often as her family might have liked.

PEACH TAPIOCA PUDDING

Soak ½ pint of tapioca in ½ pint of cold water for several hours. Fill a baking dish about half full of canned peaches, without the sirup, sprinkle the peaches with sugar and bake for half an hour. Add ½ pint of peach sirup to the tapioca, some boiling water and sugar; boil until it is perfectly clear, pour it over the peaches, and bake slowly for another half hour. Served with sugar and cream when cold.

This popular 19th century dessert can quickly be made on top of the stove by using minute or quick-cooking tapioca.

½ cup juice from canned peaches
1-½ cups water
¼ cup minute or quick-cooking tapioca

½ cup sugar
¼ teaspoon salt
2 cups sliced canned peaches, drained

Combine peach juice, water, tapioca, sugar, and salt in top of double boiler. Blend well. Cook, stirring frequently until tapioca is clear. Fold in drained peaches and cook 1 minute longer. Remove from heat. Serve in sherbet glasses. Top with whipped cream. Makes 6 servings.

MRS. RANLETT'S PUDDING SAUCE

1 cup sugar, 1-½ tablespoons of butter, 2 eggs, 1 teaspoon lemon. Beat all up to a cream, just before serving add about a tea-cup of boiling water and stir fast.

This recipe is somewhat similar to a lemon hard sauce and is quite good made with confectioners' sugar.

54

CHOCOLATE BAVARIOSE

Melt 2 ounces chocolate over hot water until glossy, stirring well, with ¼ cup sugar and ¼ cup water. Add one cup of scalded milk. Beat yolks of 3 eggs, mix with ¼ cup of sugar and cook in the hot milk and chocolate until the spoon is coated. Add ¼ package gelatine softened in ¼ cup cold water and strain into a dish standing in ice water. Flavor with one teaspoon vanilla and then stir constantly until it becomes thick, then fold in one cup of double cream beaten stiff. Have ready a mould or collolene or lard pail with a strip of parafin paper or cheese cloth about 4 inches wide lining mould with ends coming above the top. Arrange lady fingers up and down on sides a little distance apart around inside of mould up on the lining. Then pour in a little of the mixture. Straighten your cakes and then fill up. Put in a cool place an hour or more. Turn out and garnish or decorate with whipped cream and candied cherries with other fruit cut fine and blanched almonds.

We found that after a second reading we could follow the original instructions with relative ease. Our only alteration was to use ½ envelope of unflavored gelatine instead of the called for ¼ package. Pour the pudding into a 1 quart mold and chill until firm. Unmold and garnish with whipped topping and whole cherries or any other fruit you prefer. Makes 5 to 6 servings.

GOOD FRIDAY

One pint of cream let come to a boil and stir in two squares of Baker's chocolate grated. When melted add the yolks of three eggs and a teaspoon of flour well beaten. Sweeten to taste and flavor with vanilla. Cook a few minutes and pour in a glass dish. Beat the three whites of the eggs with 9 tablespoons of sugar and pile on top. The colder it is the better it is.

We used 8 tablespoons sugar, ½ teaspoon vanilla and ¼ teaspoon salt. Heat the cream until it comes to a boil. Add chocolate squares and stir until melted. Mix together egg yolks, flour, 2 tablespoons sugar, salt, and vanilla. Beat until mixture is smooth. Add this to the chocolate cream and stir until slightly thickened. Pour into individual serving dishes. Beat egg whites until foamy, then add remaining sugar, a little at a time, until stiff peaks form. Pile high on chocolate cream mixture. Makes 4 servings.

PLUM PUDDING

Plum pudding, a suet pudding, never made with plums, is a traditional Christmas dessert. On the frontier, Christmas dinners were usually looked forward to with as much anxiety as joy. The task of gathering traditional holiday foods required many weeks of searching. Often times selected foods had to be ordered from such cities as St. Louis, months in advance. The following account by Elizabeth Burt describes her first "army" Christmas dinner. It was a success in every detail, even down to the plum pudding.

"A good beef soup was an appetizing course. Then came our wee pig with an apple in his mouth, apple sauce and sweet potatoes with rice, and beans baked beautifully, and hot baking powder biscuits. Home made candy supplied the bonbons, and when the big round plum pudding was brought in with a spring of holly on the top, a burst of surprise and delight rewarded my efforts. Coffee followed as usual, but in very primitive cups. Our guests pronounced my first Christmas dinner a complete success."

RECIPE FOR PLUM PUDDING

One pound of stoned raisins, 1 pound currants, 1 pound of beef suet, chopped fine, 1 pound of grated bread crumbs or one half pound flour, 8 eggs, ¼ pound sugar—A pint of milk—one glass brandy—1 glass wine, 2 nutmegs, tablespoonful mace and cinnamon mixed, spoonful salt. Boil 6 hours.

2 cups flour	1-½ cups ground or very finely
1-½ teaspoons salt	chopped suet
½ teaspoon baking soda	2 cups raisins
½ teaspoon nutmeg	2 cups dried currants
½ teaspoon cinnamon	3 eggs, beaten
¼ teaspoon mace	¼ cup red wine
¾ cup firmly packed brown	¼ cup brandy
sugar	

Sift dry ingredients together. Combine eggs, milk, wine, and brandy. Add to dry mixture. Add suet, raisins, and currants and mix well. Pour into a greased 2-quart pudding mold. Cover mold and put on rack in large kettle. Add boiling water to come halfway up the sides of the mold. Cover kettle and steam for about 4 hours. Serve hot with a brandy hard sauce, or rum sauce. Makes 10 servings.

MRS. MILNOR'S BLACKBERRY PUDDING

2 cups brown sugar, ⅓ cup butter, 4 eggs, 4 cups flour, 1 cup milk, 3 teaspoons of baking powder. Stir in a box of blackberries, or other fruit, and steam 3 hours. This is equally good baked ¾ of an hour.

Sauce: 1 cup sugar, ½ cup butter, 2 eggs, ½ cup boiling water. Mix sugar and butter, then add yolks of eggs, then water boiling five minutes over tea kettle, and just before sending to the table add the well beaten whites.

Blackberries or brambles, as they were sometimes called, were first thought to be weeds, and not worth the time and effort to pull them up. But gradually, they became more popular, and today are considered one of the finest fruits cultivated in the United States. In this recipe we used 2 cups frozen blackberries (partially thawed) and margarine instead of butter, but altered none of the other ingredients. Our procedure for making the pudding was as follows: Combine dry ingredients. Add eggs, milk, and margarine. Mix at medium speed of electric mixer for 1 minute. Fold in blackberries. Pour mixture into buttered 3 quart baking dish. Bake at 350° for 1 hour. Serve warm. Makes 12 servings.

For the sauce we creamed the sugar and margarine and then followed the original procedure. We found that although the sauce was good, the pudding was equally delicious served with ice cream.

kettle

CHOCOLATE CREAM PUDDING

Put 2 ounces Bakers Chocolate in a pan, and set in hot water to melt. Add 1 pint hot milk or cream, ½ cup sugar, stir until well mixed, and add a teaspoon of vanilla. Moisten two tablespoons of cornstarch and add. Cook until smooth and thick, and then stir in quickly the well beaten yolks of four eggs and pour all into a serving dish. Beat the 4 whites and add 4 tablespoons powdered sugar. Heap over the chocolate and dust thickly with powdered sugar and brown.

Combine chocolate (2 squares unsweetened), milk, and sugar in a saucepan. Stir constantly over medium heat until well blended. Mix 3 tablespoons (instead of the 2 originally called for) cornstarch with ¼ cup cold water. Add to chocolate mixture and cook until smooth and thick. Quickly stir in beaten egg yolks and bring to a boil. Add vanilla and remove from heat. Pour mixture into a 1-½ quart casserole. Beat egg whites with powdered sugar until stiff. Spread on pudding, covering top completely. Bake in a 400° oven for 5 minutes or until top is lightly browned. Makes 4 servings.

GRANDMOTHER TILSBY'S CRACKER PUDDING
as made by her on thanksgiving days
Receipt taken from Aunt Lucinda Whittemore's Book
August 25, 1872, Hancock, New Hampshire

9 Boston crackers. 1 pound of raisins. 6 eggs. 1 teacup of sugar. Salt and cinnamon. To be made in a 3 quart dish after all other ingredients are in fill with milk. Butter the dish well. Sprinkle in the crackers, after being well pounded, next the raisins, sugar, salt and spice. Beat the eggs, never stirring after putting together. Bake 1-½ hours.

Substitution of Graham crackers for "Boston crackers" gives this recipe an especially fine base. One-half teaspoon salt, 1 teaspoon cinnamon, and ¾ to 1 cup sugar were used. We followed the original recipe in all other details, baking it for 1-½ hours at 325°. Similar to custard in texture, it tastes very much like Bread Pudding. Makes 12 servings.

TO PRESERVE PEACHES IN CANS
Mrs. Flagg's Recipe

Pare and quarter the peaches and fill the cans, as full as you can without crowding them. For the syrup take one pint of loaf sugar to a quart of water and boil five minutes, skimming until free from motes. Pour it while boiling upon the peaches, then solder the cover on, having made a small hole in the top with a nail or fork, for the air to escape. Take a washboiler or the largest vehicle of the kind you possess and put there in, as many cans, easily placed on the bottom. Pour on cold water until it comes within an inch of the top of the cans. Let the water come to a boil and boil about five minutes, then take the cans out and seal the orifice in the top, with all possible dispatch. Blackberries are put up in the same manner. The peaches should be perfectly ripe, but no more.

APPLE PUDDING

5 apples, chopped, 1 cup raisins (stoned), 1 cup sugar, 1 cup sweet milk, 1 cup flour, ½ cup butter, 2 eggs, little salt. Butter and sugar worked together. Stir until light. Bake one hour and eat with sauce, made of ½ cup butter, 1 cup sugar. Beat well and flavor.

Cream butter and sugar until light. Add eggs, one at a time, and beat well. Sift flour with ¼ teaspoon salt and add to creamed mixture alternately with milk. Fold in raisins and apples. Pour into an 8 by 3 inch baking dish. Set dish in a pan of water and bake at 350° for one hour.

For the sauce: Beat the ½ cup butter until light and fluffy. Gradually beat in the one cup of sugar and continue beating until mixture is smooth. Add 1 teaspoon of vanilla for flavoring, and cut into pudding while it is still hot. Serve warm. Makes 8 servings. As this pudding is very rich you may prefer to serve it with a lighter sauce or no sauce at all.

PRESERVING EGGS FOR WINTER — Pack in a clean vessel with small end down, strewing bran between each layer. Then place one or two thicknesses of brown paper on top and cover about one inch thick with salt. Cover close or keep in a cool place.

SISTER FANNIE'S INDIAN PUDDING

One cup (not quite full) of molasses, 2/3 cup corn meal, one egg, heaping teaspoon of butter or tablespoon of suet, salt, ginger or cinnamon to taste, all beaten together. Full quart sweet milk, put on to boil and these ingredients stirred in. Take from fire and add nearly two-thirds cup cold milk. Pour into a baking dish on to lumps of butter. Bake one hour. <u>*Extra Good.*</u>

¾ cup molasses	½ teaspoon salt
2/3 cup yellow cornmeal	1 teaspoon ginger
2 eggs, beaten	4-2/3 cups milk
1 tablespoon butter	

Heat 3 cups of milk in top part of double boiler over boiling water. Mix 1 cup milk and the cornmeal. Stir into hot milk. Combine molasses, beaten eggs, butter, salt, and ginger and add to cornmeal-milk mixture. Cook over low heat until mixture thickens slightly. Remove from heat and add remaining milk. Pour into buttered 2-quart casserole and bake in preheated 275° oven for 2 hours. Makes 8 servings.

This pudding may be served warm or cool with whipped cream or ice cream.

A German medical journal asserts that boiled milk is more easily and rapidly digested than unboiled milk and that the curds are softer. — FOOTE'S HEALTH MONTHLY

HOUSEHOLD HINTS AND HOME REMEDIES

The following section on home remedies and household hints is included primarily as a matter of interest rather than use. Cookbooks of the 19th century contained chapters on remedies for the sick, and proper methods of cleaning house. These helpful 'words of wisdom' were followed implicitly, especially by women living on the frontier. It was not until the early 20th century that American women could obtain a book entirely devoted to cooking.

Most western military forts had a post surgeon, but the availability of medicines was somewhat lacking. On the frontier, women prepared their own concoctions for the treatment of everything from insect bites to rheumatism. Women also made their own soap, toothpaste, and even perfumes.

Mrs. Grierson faithfully read the 'Household Hints' columns which appeared in the newspapers. She regularly clipped articles and pasted them into her recipe book. Write-ups covered a wide variety of subjects from "how to keep boots from cracking," to "restoring the hair after illness." Many of these pearls of advice are not applicable today, but they give us an interesting and amusing look into the past.

heater

MOTHER'S COUGH SYRUP

Half an ounce of Horehound, one ounce of licorice root, and half a tea-cup of Flax-seed. Boil them in three pints of water down to a pint, and sweeten well with honey or loaf sugar, add sufficient spirit to keep it if you please.

ANOTHER COUGH SYRUP

Take a small handful of hops and some old field balsam and some horehound, and make a strong tea; strain and put as much molasses as tea; boil down to about one-half. To be taken before eating and before going to bed.

"HOOPING" COUGH
Mother's Remedy

Dissolve a sample of salts of tartar in a quarter of a pint of water, add to it 10 grains of Cochineal finely powdered, sweeten with loaf sugar or honey until a syrup. This recipe is from an old Scotch Doctor of Concord, N.H.

COLD CURE

One ounce each of licorice root, thoroughwort, flax seed, and slippery elm bark. Cut the elm bark and licorice root up fine, mix with the water; steep slowly for ten hours. Strain, and add to the sirup one pound of loaf sugar and one pint of molasses; boil a few minutes and bottle. Take a tablespoonful four times a day.

CANKER SORES

The following recipe appeared in the POULTRY MONTHLY. For canker, paint twice daily with perchloride of iron the inside of the mouth and touch the sores outside with lunar caustic. Give twice each week as much epsom salts as will lie on a quarter.

TOOTH ACHE

Two drams of nitrous spirits of ether mixed with 5 drams of alum, reduced to an impalpable powder apply on with cotton.

TO CLEAN THE INSIDE OF IRON POTS AND PANS

The best way to clean the inside of old iron pots and pans is to fill them with water in which a few ounces of washing soda is dissolved and set them on the fire. Let the water boil until the inside of the pot looks clean.

GUNPOWDER BURN

For a gunpowder burn, keep the wounds wet with a mixture of linseed oil and lime water for three days, and then apply vaseline to heal.

A HEALING OINTMENT

Take the inside bark of sweet elder, boil to a strong infusion; strain it, then add equal parts of beeswax, and mutton tallow; say to ½ pint of the liquid a piece of mutton tallow and beeswax each the size of a hens egg; simmer until the water is out. If a softer ointment is desired, use fresh butter instead of mutton tallow. Here you have a recipe for an ointment which is invaluable as a healing remedy for sores, cuts, chilblains, and sores of all kinds, and especially excellent for burns.

NEURALGIA
from "Household Hints"

A lady who has been troubled with the neuralgia in her head, used a bag of hot oats at night as a pillow. She says: "heat the oats in a kettle over the fire, or in a pan in your oven. I have never been troubled with neuralgia any place but in my head so I cannot say how beneficial it would be for neuralgia in other parts of the body." Another cure is drinking hot lemonade.

CARE OF SILK

Never use a brush; it injures the goods. Instead wipe carefully with the face of a soft piece of velvet. Shake the velvet occasionally and wipe between every plait if you would preserve your garment and have it retain its new look.

PASTE FOR SCRAP BOOKS

Use a piece of alum the size of a walnut in one pint of boiling water. To this add two tablespoons flour made smooth in cold water and a few drops of oil of cloves, letting all come to a boil and put into a canning jar or any similar vehicle. It will keep for months.

COLOGNE
John's Recipe
6 oz.

Oil of Lavender — 2 drachmas
Oil of Lemon — 2 drachmas
Oil of Bergamot — 1 drachmas
Oil of Rosemary — 2 drachmas
Oil of Cinnamon — 8 drops
Tincture of Musk — 10 drops
Oil of Cloves — 8 drops
Oil of Rose — 8 drops

The above articles to put into a bottle with one pint of rectified spirits of wine.

cologne

TOOTH WASH

Dissolve 2 ounces Borax in 3 pints of warm water. Before the water is quite cold add 1 teaspoon tinct myrrh, and one tablespoon of spirits of camphor. Bottle and use a wine glass to one-half pint of warm water. It preserves and beautifies the teeth.

HARSH SOAP

Mother's Recipe

One gallon of hot water to one box of concentrated lye and two gallons of water to five pounds of grease.

SOFT SOAP

Fry out fourteen pounds of grease; to this add ten pounds potash dissolved in just boiling water enough to cover the lumps. In two or three days pour the mixture several pailfuls of boiling water. (Be careful to use boiling water, as that cooks it). Keep on adding water as fast as the soap thickens until your barrel is full of nice, sweet soap. It must be stirred <u>hard</u> every time the water is put into the barrel until it is entirely mixed.

HAIR DYE

½ *drachma sugar of lead*   2 *ounces rose water*
1 *drachma lac sulphur*   1 *ounce bay rum*
2 *ounces glycerine*

Put the sugar of lead and sulphur into a pint of boiling rain water and let it stand till cold. Then add the remaining ingredients after having mixed the glycerine thoroughly with the rum and rose water.

TO PRODUCE A GOOD GLOSS ON LINEN

Pour a pint of boiling water upon two ounces of gum arabic, cover, and let stand over night; add a spoonful to the starch.

TO FADE COLORED GOODS OR IRON RUST

*Two ounces chloride of lime, two quarts of boiling water and two
quarts of cold water. Put in a basket overnight, then lay on grass
if the color is not out.*

CLEANING FLUID
for
WOOLEN GOODS AND MARKS ON FURNITURE

4 ounces ammonia
2 ounces alcohol
2 ounces ether

4 ounces white castile soap
2 ounces glycerine

*Cut soap fine, dissolve in one quart water over the fire. Add four
quarts water. When nearly cold add other ingredients. This will
make eight quarts and will cost 75 cents. Put into a bottle and
cork. To wash a dress: to a pail of luke-warm water, put a cup
of the fluid, shake well, and rinse in plenty of water.*

TO RESTORE HAIR AFTER AN ILLNESS

*Equal parts of best brandy and strong black tea, shaken well to-
gether and rubbed well into the roots of the hair once daily, will
usually restore the hair after long illness. Be careful not to scratch
or irritate the scalp with rough combing and brushing. The mixture should be made at least once in three days even in cool weather.*

TO REMOVE FRUIT STAINS

*When a napkin or table cloth gets stained with fruit or berries, if
boiling hot water is poured on the stained spot, it will rinse out
entirely, but if it should be overlooked and go into the wash, soaking the spots in warm new milk will remove them. For weak
stains in cotton goods, warm new milk is the remedy, if applied
immediately. On woolen or worsted garments, a little spirits of
turpentine, rubbed on with a woolen cloth, will take the ink all
out; then wash out with pure warm water.*

TO WASH FLANNEL

Never rub soap upon it. Make a suds by dissolving the soap in warm water; rinse in warm water. Very cold or hot water will shrink flannel. Shake it out several minutes before hanging to dry. Blankets can be washed in the same way.

HAIR PRESERVATIVE

To prevent hair from falling out, take 1 teaspoon of salt, 30 grains of quinine, and a pint of bay rum. Rub the hair thoroughly every night. Another remedy is to take a handful of Southern wood leaves, cover them with alcohol, and let them stand till the strength is extracted. Add 1 teaspoon of this to ⅓ cup water, and wet the scalp thoroughly once a day.

HOW TO CURE WARTS

It is now fairly established that the common wart, which is so unsightly and often proliferous on the hands and face can be easily removed by small doses of sulphate magnesia taken internally.

TO KEEP MOTHS FROM FURS

An experienced fur dealer says that oil of peppermint is the best thing to keep moths and all insects from furs.

TO REMOVE GREASE FROM A CARPET

Buckwheat batter spread upon a grease spot in an ingrain carpet will absorb the grease. It can be readily scraped off when dry.

coal hod, shovel / tongs

CREAKING BOOTS

The noise is caused by the rubbing together of two surfaces of leather in the soles. It usually disappears when the boots are somewhat worn. Soak the soles thoroughly with warm water and while wet apply a liberal coating of oil or grease and dry it in. This will add considerably to the wear of the boots, and cure all but the most inveterate cases of creaking.

TO REMOVE DIRT FROM THE EYE

Take a hog's bristle, double so as to form a loop. Lift the eyelid and gently insert the loop over the eyeball, which will cause no disagreeable feeling. Now close the lid down upon the bristle, which may now be withdrawn. The dirt will surely be on the bristle.

TO REMOVE SCORCHES FROM LINEN
Alice Bishop's Recipe

Scorches made by heated flatirons can be removed from linen by spreading over the cloth a paste made of the juice pressed from two onions, one-half ounce white soap, two ounces fuller's earth and one-half pint vinegar. Mix boil well, and cool before using.

CHAPPED HANDS

The surest remedy for chapped hands is to rinse well after washing with soap and dry them thoroughly by applying Indian meal.

TO MAKE TINCTURE OF ROSES

Take leaves of common roses, or better still, the damask rose. Place them, without pressing in a good bottle, pour good spirits upon them, close the bottle, and let it stand until required for use. This tincture will keep for years and yield a perfume little inferior to attar of roses. A few drops of it will suffice to impregnate the atmosphere of a room with a delicious odor.

Background materials and direct quotes were taken from the following sources:

American Heritage Cookbook by the editors of American Heritage, American Heritage Publishing Co., 1964.

Bullock, Helen. *The Williamsburg Art of Cookery or Accomplished Gentlewoman's Companion.* Colonial Williamsburg, 1966.

Fougera, Katherine Gibson. *With Custer's Cavalry.* Caldwell, Idaho, 1942.

Grierson, Benjamin H. "Lights and Shadows of Life." An unpublished manuscript. Illinois State Historic Library.

Grierson Manuscript Collection — Fort Davis National Historic Site.

Holbrook, Captain L. R. *The Mess Officer's Assistant.* Mounted Service School Press, 1909.

Johnson, Lawrence A. *Over the Counter and on the Shelf, Country Storekeeping in America 1620-1920.* Bonanza Books, 1961.

Lane, Lydia Spencer. *I Married A Soldier or Old Days in the Old Army.* Albuquerque, 1964.

Magoffin, Susan Shelby. *Down the Santa Fe Trail and into Mexico.* Edited by Stella M. Drumm. New Haven, 1962.

Mattes, Merrill J. *Indians, Infants and Infantry, Andrew and Elizabeth Burt on the Frontier.* Denver, 1960.

Roe, Frances M. A. *Army Letters of An Officer's Wife, 1871-1888.* New York, 1909.

Russell, Mrs. Hal. *Land of Enchantment, Memoirs of Marian Russell along the Santa Fe Trail.* Edited by Garnet M. Brayer, Evanston, Illinois, 1954.

Russell, Mrs. Hal. *Settler Mac and the Charmed Quarter-Section.* Denver, 1956.

Sanderson, Captain James M. *Camp Fires and Camp Cooking or Culinary Hints for the Soldier.* Washington, 1862.

Sibbald, John R. "Army Women of the West." The American West, Vol. III, No. 2 (Spring, 1966).

Summerhayes, Martha. *Vanished Arizona, Recollections of my Army Life.* Chicago, 1939.

Tyree, Marion Cabell. *Housekeeping in Old Virginia.* Reprint edition of original book published in 1879. Louisville, 1965.

INDEX